After Hours

Arts & Leisure in America

Timely Reports to Keep
Journalists, Scholars and the Public
Abreast of Developing Issues, Events and Trends

Editorial Research Reports
Published by Congressional Quarterly Inc.
1414 22nd Street, N.W.
Washington, D.C. 20037

About the Cover

The cover was designed by Art Director Richard Pottern

Editor, Hoyt Gimlin
Associate Editor, Martha V. Gottron
Editorial Assistants, Leah Klumph, Elizabeth Furbush
Production Manager, I. D. Fuller
Assistant Production Manager, Maceo Mayo

Library of Congress Cataloging in Publication Data

Main entry under title

After hours.

Reprints of reports that originally appeared in Editorial Research Reports.
Bibliography: p.
Includes index.
1. Leisure — United States — Addresses, essays, lectures.
I. Editorial research reports. II. Congressional Quarterly, inc.
GV53.A67   1985   790′.01′350973   85-25516
ISBN 0-87187-371-0

Contents

Foreword

Americans take their pleasure seriously. They spent at least $200 billion last year on leisure-time activities, which include everything from baseball to theater. Obviously, what is one person's pleasure may well be another's livelihood. Several reports in this collection explore the business side of leisure. Take tourism, for example. The Commerce Department calculates that Americans spent nearly $25 billion last year on airline travel and lodging during vacations and other personal trips. In 39 of the 50 states, tourism is one of the three biggest sources of revenue.

Or look at book publishing. Retail book sales last year went well over two billion and brought in nearly $13 billion. The public's seemingly insatiable appetite for sports events has translated into big business for television — and for the teams, professional leagues and college conferences that sell broadcast rights. The average 30 second commercial aired in prime time during ABC's coverage of the 1984 Olympic Games sold for $260,000.

Yet the economics of leisure tells only one part of the story. Many of the popular pastimes reflect the diversity of this country's people and their search for historical roots. The author of a report on dining finds that many of the nation's trend-setting chefs are concentrating on its culinary heritage, especially regional cooking. The fashion world has learned that American women no longer blindly follow designer dictates and that they look beyond Paris to London, Japan, Italy and New York for ideas. Some of the most critically acclaimed country musicians are working traditional elements into their music. Preservation and restoration of old houses and commercial buildings is widespread. Architect Philip Johnson says his profession is showing "a new pluralism ... a new willingness to use history" in its designs. While the reports collected together in this volume delve into only a few of the many ways Americans spend their leisure time, we believe they are representative and hope they are informative.

Martha V. Gottron
Editor

October 1985
Washington, D.C.

DINING
IN
AMERICA

by

Robert Benenson

**May 18
1 9 8 4**

DINING IN AMERICA

F INE DINING, once the province of the rich, has become an obsession for millions of middle-class Americans. Tens of thousands are enrolled in cooking classes, learning everything from how to boil water to how to make Chinese wontons. Culinary schools are flooded with applications. Newspapers have expanded their food sections. Celebrity, once accorded only to well-known television cooks and authors such as James Beard and Julia Child, now accrues to chefs of individual restaurants.

Currently a great debate in the food world concerns the definition of the New American Cuisine. One faction takes a "Roots"-like approach, emphasizing America's culinary heritage, particularly regional cooking. The other faction borrows its style from French nouvelle cuisine, preparing simple, lightly cooked dishes from unusual but American-produced meats, vegetables and dairy products.

This schism may liven up conversations among the condo crowd and the soon-to-be-affluent "yumpies" (for young upwardly mobile persons, or professionals). But this growing interest in "gourmet" food has had little effect on the tastes of the average American. "We're talking about a very small percentage of the population that's involved in all this upscale eating, and that's not going to change," said *New York Times* restaurant critic Marian Burros.[1] While culinarians were arguing the relative merits of Cajun gumbo vs. smoked salmon pizza, the rest of America was turning a fast-food advertising slogan, "Where's The Beef?" into an instant cliché.

Fast-food, or limited-menu, restaurants continue to be the fastest growing segment of the $100 billion commercial food and drink industry. Lifestyle trends in the post-World War II era — particularly big increases in the numbers of working women and single-person households — helped the late McDonald's magnate Ray A. Kroc become not only a multimillionaire but an industry prophet. Even many committed weekend cooks rely on fast food to help them through their busy schedules of work,

---

[1] Persons quoted in this report were interviewed by the author unless otherwise indicated.

exercise and socializing. Fast-food executives, who traditionally have made their pitch to families, are beginning to target their efforts toward this adult, quality-conscious market.

Fast-food restaurants are also responding to the widespread interest in nutrition and diet. Many fast-food chains have added salad bars to counter criticisms of their heavy emphasis on meat, fried foods and sugary drinks.

Although Americans are dining out more than ever, they still spend almost two-thirds of their food budgets at the grocery store. The American consumer may describe nutrition and weight control as main concerns, but government and industry figures show a mixed picture. Sales of fresh produce have jumped in recent years. Many supermarkets are providing a wider variety of fresh vegetables, meat and fish for the taste- or diet-conscious. "Light," low-sodium and "natural" foods are being mass-marketed. But diet concerns have hardly transformed the marketplace. Food manufacturers are competing fiercely for a share of the growing packaged cookie market.

Influence of the French Nouvelle Cuisine

That many of today's best American chefs have taken their inspiration from the French nouvelle cuisine ("new cooking") trend is not surprising. France has been considered the mecca of culinary arts throughout American history. Thomas Jefferson brought a French chef (Julien Lemaire) into the White House in 1801. Many of the words associated with fine dining — haute cuisine, gourmet, connoisseur — are French in origin, as are the more common "chef" and "menu."

Most lists of great American eating places are still dominated by French restaurants: New York's Lutece, Washington's Le Lion D'Or and suburban Chicago's Le Français, for example. Trademarks of fine French cooking — crepes, souffles, quiche, mousse — are now widely imitated in American kitchens, at least in part thanks to Julia Child, well known as television's "French Chef."

The name most commonly associated with classical, or traditional, French cuisine is that of Georges Auguste Escoffier (1846-1935). The "king of cooks" was chef at fine restaurants in Paris, Monte Carlo and London. One of the memorable dishes he developed is peach Melba. But Escoffier is best known for reorganizing restaurant kitchens under a series of sub-chefs and for establishing new rules for cooking French haute cuisine.

The classical French meal featured many courses and an abundance of rich, heavy sauces. "If you worked in a professional [French] kitchen, each day you made and used a gallon of hollandaise sauce and tossed it into everything," Craig Claiborne, the *New York Times* food editor, wrote recently.[2] Claiborne also noted that during Escoffier's era people's caloric needs were greater — there were no automobiles or mass transit and few other labor-saving devices. Such food is inappropriate for our modern times, he said; "We are far more health- and weight-conscious, and our bodies demand a lighter style of cooking. We eat less salt and our intake of fat has decreased."

By the 1970s, innovative chefs such as Paul Bocuse, Roger Verge and Alain Chapel had developed a new style of French cooking. Characterized by simple sauces of butter and herbs and

unique combinations of meats, vegetables and seasonings, the style was dubbed "nouvelle cuisine." Claiborne, who called nouvelle cuisine "the greatest innovation in the world of food since the food processor," compared the "traditional cassoulet with all that pork rind, preserved goose, pork belly and sausages," and the sauerkraut "with its goose fat, streaky bacon, ham and sausages," to such light, delicate nouvelle standards as "fresh salmon in sorrel sauce, duck livers with celery root, a simple dish of sole with chives, striped bass wrapped in green lettuce leaves, and a simple grilled chicken. . . ." Style is nearly as important as taste in nouvelle creations; the food is arranged artistically on the plate with an eye to both color and texture.

The move away from the rules of haute cuisine also freed young American chefs to compete with their French counterparts as innovators. Cooks created dishes that utilized traditional foodstuffs, many of which had been important in America's early years, but which had faded from currency as the nation became more urbanized and food tastes more standardized. Game, such as venison and quail, began to reappear on menus, as did numerous varieties of shellfish, herbs and vegetables. Meats were often grilled over mesquite wood.

The trend was popularized first in California, where chefs such as Alice Waters, owner of Berkeley's Chez Panisse, plied

[2] Craig Claiborne, "Nouvelle Cuisine: Here To Stay," *The New York Times Magazine*, Dec. 18, 1983.

their trade. A recent article by Roman Czajkowsky in *Nation's Restaurant News* called Waters the "mother of California cuisine," and listed a sampler of her creations: boned tenderloin of pork marinated in coriander, juniper berries and herbs, rubbed with olive oil and grilled; fresh shellfish grilled over mesquite charcoal; and ravioli stuffed with mashed potatoes and garlic.[3] As the trend spread and came to be described by some food writers as the New American cuisine, the use of domestic ingredients became almost dogma to some chefs. Larry Forgione of An American Place in New York is among those who use only American-grown ingredients.

Failure to Heed Fundamentals Criticized

The traditions of Escoffier are looked down upon by some nouvelle advocates. Czajkowsky's article called restaurants run by Waters and those she has influenced "part of the growing group of this country's fine dining meccas where Monsieur Escoffier would not be let through the door." But the French master still has his disciples. Ferdinand Metz, president of the Culinary Institute of America in Hyde Park, N.Y., said that the fundamentals laid down by Escoffier are "always the basis of everything that we do."[4] He added, "Classical is not a basic form of cooking, it is drawing on the basics reflecting what society wanted at the time. Nouvelle is still drawing on the basics, but reflecting a new kind of recognition."

Food critic Mimi Sheraton agrees with Metz that dishes created with disregard to the basics can lead to conflict rather than harmony in tastes. Sheraton is especially critical of nouvelle and New American cooks who apply sweet flavorings, such as raspberry vinegar and confit of onions (a sort of onion marmalade), to their creations. "A lot of young people who do not have a classical background, they have not eaten a lot, they have not had a lot of taste experiences, think anything goes if they like it," Sheraton said. "If they don't have the base, and just say, 'There are no rules,' you get a lot of very terrible food."

The new cuisines have engendered pretensions that can be taken to extremes. Metz criticized the practice of "giving you two little medallions on a big plate, and a lot of sauce and these fancy gyrations and drawings in the sauce, or putting a kiwi [fruit] on things and saying, 'Guess what? Now it's all nouvelle.'" Some restaurants also go overboard with their elaborate descriptions of each dish. "I sometimes fall off the chair listening to the captain go on with what's in a dish, as they do that

---

[3] *Nation's Restaurant News,* February 13, 1984.
[4] The formal French restaurant at the Culinary Institute is named for Escoffier, whose portrait hangs in Metz's office. The institute is the largest and best-known cooking school in the United States.

crazy recitation," Sheraton said. " 'You put in woodland mushrooms, and you put in white raisins, and you put in mangoes and you put in corn kernels,' and it goes on and on and on, and you feel full just listening to it."

 **Regional Cooking**

MODIFIED nouvelle cuisine has competition for the title of New American cuisine. According to *Nation's Restaurant News* editor Paul Frumkin, food professionals are divided into two camps: the innovators who say "American cuisine is like America, and we can incorporate just about anything we want, because America's so diverse," and the purists who say "it really has to be from colonial cookbooks and it has to be turkeys, and it has to be corn, and it has to be cranberries, all the unique, very traditional things." The purists are helping spread the gospel of American regional cooking.

Some regional dishes are familiar all over the country; most Americans have stumbled over some local imitation of barbecued ribs or New England clam chowder. But many chefs are demanding authenticity and using top-grade ingredients. The trend was given a big boost in 1983, when regional food was featured at the Western nations' economic summit conference in Williamsburg, Va. The menu included North Carolina-style spicy barbecue, deep-fried catfish and hush puppies, Louisiana gumbo and coleslaw, and Key lime pie.

Restaurants celebrating the specialties of single regions have sprouted in far-off reaches. Among the popular restaurants in New York, for example, are Sidewalkers (Maryland steamed crab); Carolina (mesquite-grilled ribs and chicken); the Cottonwood Cafe (Texas-style pork chops, chicken fried steak, mashed potatoes); and Texarkana (Cajun and Creole specialties such as gumbo and jambalaya).

Cajun cooking, until recently little known beyond New Orleans and the rural backwaters inhabited by people of French Acadian ancestry, is one of the hottest food crazes — literally and figuratively. When Paul Prudhomme, best known of New Orleans' Cajun cooks, opened a version of his K-Paul's Louisiana Kitchen in San Francisco for four weeks last summer, people formed block-long queues waiting to sample the spicy delicacies.

Some writers attribute the upsurge in regional cooking to a combination of sentiment and national pride. "The roots of regional cooking are entangled with the nation's history and the national psyche," Joan Nathan and Elizabeth Sahatjian wrote in *Cuisine* magazine. "A fresh apple pie, Tennessee barbecued ribs, Boston clam chowder, New Orleans jambalaya, New York City's hot pastrami sandwiches, the five-alarm chilies of Texas — they all resonate in the heart as well as the stomach." Others note that Americans are traveling more than ever, experiencing firsthand the specialties of other regions and bringing home a desire for more. Some of the fervor for spicy sauces and the stick-to-your-ribs heartiness of much regional fare may be a backlash against the more effete nouvelle cuisine.[5]

Culinary Institute President Metz cautions that regional cooking, like nouvelle cuisine, can be carried to extremes, especially if it means creating dishes far from the source of the ingredients that make them unique. "There's no reason why we need to bring things all the way across, there's so much in each region that we can draw upon," Metz said. "There will always be the opportunity to make dishes from different regions, but not at the expense of trucking ingredients across the country, making it very expensive and unreasonable. In other words, if you can, do it, but if it creates a problem, you don't need to."

New Prestige Accorded Chefs and Cooking

The wave of interest in American gastronomy has created a new breed of celebrity: the "superstar chef." Luminaries such as Wolfgang Puck, chef-owner of Spago in Los Angeles and former chef of that city's exclusive Ma Maison, and Paul Prudhomme in New Orleans have been profiled in magazines and newspapers and on television.

Cooking has only recently become an honored line of work in this country. Because of America's longstanding culinary Francophilia, American chefs stood in the shadows of their French counterparts. When he came to the United States from his native West Germany in the early 1960s, Metz said, cooking was regarded as "menial labor."

Today, cooking has become a sought-after, and at the top levels well-paying, line of work. The Culinary Institute has 1,850 students enrolled in its two-year program and receives twice that many applications for admission. "At Friday's graduation, parents [who are doctors] came up to me and said how proud

---

[5] In a Jan. 10, 1984, *Wall Street Journal* article entitled, "Stir the Buffalo Stew, Zeke; the Gourmets are Waiting in Line," reporter Trish Hall referred to the trend as "nouvelle cowboy." Buffalo is indeed an item in demand, which should probably be regarded as a surge rather than a resurgence. While many Indian tribes subsisted on buffalo, white settlers rarely ate the animals they slaughtered to the point of near-extinction.

they were ... that their son or daughter had graduated, had found a profession they really love," Metz said. "Ten years ago, they would not have attended graduation."

The New York Restaurant School in Manhattan enjoys a similar situation, according to Executive Director William Liederman. Of the 400 students enrolled in the school's 18-week course of cooking, baking and small restaurant management, most are career-switchers. "The average age is 30," said Liederman. "They're ex-lawyers, accountants, people from advertising, nurses, we have an ex-priest." Virtually all remain enrolled for the duration of the course.

Mimi Sheraton said the best thing about the new interest in food "is that it has made cooking seem like a worthwhile profession for young people." The biggest negative, she said, is the tendency among some young chefs to be "messianic" about their trade, insisting that their creations are infallible and refusing to make modifications in a dish at the diner's request. "I think there has to be a little more give on the part of some of the young restaurateurs who think they are going to teach the public how to eat," Sheraton said.

Popularity of Foreign Foods on the Increase

The American palate has hardly turned entirely chauvinistic. Foreign cuisines are also growing in popularity. "John Q. Public is growing more adventurous," New York State Restaurant Association Chairman Stuart Levin said.[6] A survey conducted by the National Restaurant Association last summer found that 94 percent of the respondents had eaten Italian food in a restaurant, 89 percent had sampled Chinese fare, and 88 percent had tried Mexican food (though culinary purists will note that many people limited their selections to the ubiquitous pizza and spaghetti, Americanized Chinese dishes such as chop suey and chow mein, and tacos).

Immigrant groups have added elements of their national foods to America's culinary vocabulary throughout its history: pasta, smorgasbord, delicatessen, frankfurter, and goulash are just a few examples. But while each ethnic group has made its contribution to the "melting pot," most have been able to preserve their culinary roots.

The authenticity of foreign cuisines is obviously greater in cities with large ethnic-American populations, such as New York, Washington, Chicago, San Francisco and Los Angeles. New immigrant groups continue to add to these cities' ample selections. For instance, the influx of recent refugee groups has

---

[6] Quoted in *Nation's Restaurant News*, Jan. 2, 1984.

resulted in the opening of Ethiopian, Afghan, Cuban, Salvadoran and Vietnamese restaurants in Washington.

Not all of the popular foreign cuisines are highly seasoned; Japan's sushi (raw fish) is an example. But as in the barbecue and Cajun crazes, some Americans have plunged into the spiciest of foreign cuisines: Indian, Thai, regional Chinese. Mimi Sheraton, an aficionado of spicy food, is skeptical of persons who claim to be fire-eaters. "There are a lot of people who like food truly hotly seasoned, and then there are others who think that's the way to order it now, but they don't really like it that way," Sheraton said. She related the story of an Indian restaurateur who, having had several diners complain that the food they had ordered as very spicy was too spicy, required patrons to say "four very's" (very, very, very, very spicy) before he would serve food that way.

Grocery Shopping

T HE COOKING MANIA has affected the way supermarkets do business. "Upscaling," an invented word for the targeting of sales to the upper-income brackets, is in. Many supermarkets have added in-store bakeries and expanded their deli sections to include specialty items among their usual selections of cold cuts, processed cheeses and salads. Fresh fish sections are springing up, even in markets that had earlier removed them. The dollar value of fresh seafood sold in grocery stores increased 13.1 percent in 1981 and 7.0 percent in 1982.[7] "Gourmet" supermarkets, such as Giant's "Something Special" in the wealthy Washington suburb of McLean, Va., and Shopwell's "Food Emporium" stores in the New York City area, are becoming more common in affluent communities.

A walk through the aisles of many supermarkets will demonstrate that Americans have become more broad-minded about what they eat. A chain store in Alexandria, Va., recently carried six types of lettuce besides iceberg — red leaf, green leaf, escarole, Boston, romaine and bibb. Other selections included alfalfa and bean sprouts, snow peas, shallots, watercress, artichokes, leeks, fresh dill and hydroponic (grown in water) cucumbers. Other markets in communities with large Asian populations carry bok choy, napa lettuce and other Oriental

---

[7] Figures from the consumer expenditure survey released annually in September by *Supermarket Business* magazine.

vegetables; stores with Latin American customers carry cilantro, chorizos and a variety of hot chili peppers.

The United Fresh Fruit and Vegetable Association distributes leaflets to encourage grocers to stock and consumers to buy specialty fruits and vegetables. These include chayote, a squashlike vegetable, pronounced shy-o-tay; daikon, a white Oriental radish; nopales or cactus leaves; salsify, a parsniplike root; and sunchoke or Jerusalem artichoke, a knobby root vegetable that was a favorite of the early American colonists. Among the fruits are cherimoya, a South American fruit that has a taste described as "reminiscent of strawberry, banana and pineapple all in one"; plantain, which looks like a big, bruised banana but which must be cooked before eating; prickly pear, the fruit of a type of cactus; and ugli fruit, an appropriately named hybrid of grapefruit and tangerine with a rough, mottled skin and a sweet citrus taste. However, the more familiar produce remains the most popular. In 1982, per capita consumption of the three most popular vegetables — fresh potatoes, lettuce and tomatoes — was 82 pounds *(see table, p. 13)*.

Processed Foods Geared to Affluent Buyers

The fresh produce industry boomed over the last decade. Per capita fresh vegetable consumption excluding potatoes in 1982 was a record 100.9 pounds, compared with 89.1 pounds in 1972. Per capita fresh fruit consumption in 1982, 81.2 pounds excluding melons, was slightly below the 1980 record of 85.3 pounds, but was well above the 1972 figure of 74.9 pounds. Meanwhile, canned produce showed a sharp dropoff: 1982 per capita vegetable consumption (45.6 pounds) was down nearly 10 pounds from the peak year of 1979 (55.6 pounds). Canned fruit also dropped from 21.3 pounds in 1972 to 13.0 pounds in 1982.

However, the nation's big food processors — General Foods, General Mills and Campbell's, for example — have hardly been threatened with extinction. According to figures obtained from *Supermarket Business* magazine's annual consumer expenditure survey, almost three times as much money was spent in 1982 on white bread as on all other breads combined. Nearly $8 billion was spent on crackers, packaged cookies, potato chips and other snack foods. The frozen prepared food category was one of the fastest-growing; frozen dinner sales jumped 10.1 percent in 1982.

The fast-food industry *(see p. 16)* has not grown into a dominant force in American culture by accident; shoppers often choose convenience over taste in their grocery choices too. Yet new product marketing reflects the growing taste consciousness of the so-called "upscale" buyer. The star products among frozen foods are gourmet dinners such as Stouffer's Lean Cuisine, Armour's Dinner Classics and Buitoni's Classic Entrees. Swanson Foods pioneered TV dinners in 1953, but its turkey and salisbury steak classics may seem pedestrian compared with the beef sirloin tips, Yankee pot roast and chicken a l'orange of its Le Menu line.

Food writers have mixed reactions to the new products. "Take away the sophisticated packaging and, to my eye, they still look suspiciously like airplane food — though, I admit, they do taste better," wrote Bernice Kanner in *New York* magazine. But Burros of *The New York Times* was not impressed, saying, "[The food companies] may think they're better [than the original TV dinners] but my personal opinion is that they're equally unpalatable."

The packaged cookie business is undergoing a similar upscaling. While many old favorites remain popular — Nabisco sold 102 million packages of Oreos last year — the big bakers have reacted to incursions by in-store bakeries and by storefront shops specializing in chewy, all-butter cookies *(see p. 19)*. Nabisco ("Almost Home"), Duncan Hines, and Frito-Lay ("Grandma's Rich'n Chewy") are battling for market share in the "moist-and-chewy" cookie business. Again, Burros is skeptical of the quality. She says the massive scale and shelf-life requirements of the corporate bakers precludes the quality provided by the smaller, same-day-sale retail outlets. "You just can't do it on that scale, and you can't do it so that it's going to last for six months," Burros said.

Nutrition Concerns: A New Market Priority

While taste is an important consideration for shoppers, the aroused nutrition- and diet-consciousness of the American public may be having an even greater impact on marketing decisions. Numerous studies connecting high-fat, high-cholesterol diets to heart disease and cancer, and high-sodium diets to high blood pressure have changed many Americans' eating habits. Vanity as well as health account for the new weight-control consciousness.

These general health concerns have boosted some of the recent food trends. Salads and fresh vegetables are prominent on most weight-reduction diets; many fresh produce items contain large amounts of fiber, which is believed to aid digestion and reduce the risk of certain cancers. The most popular of the upscale frozen dinners are the Lean Cuisines, with their marketing emphasis on "less than 300 calories per serving."

The diet trend has resulted in the introduction of numerous products labeled "light" or "diet." Most of the time, "light" means fewer calories. There are "light" processed cheeses, salad

The Food We Eat

	Lbs./Person 1972	Lbs./Person 1982		Lbs./Person 1972	Lbs./Person 1982
Meat, Poultry			**Fresh Vegetables**		
Red meat	103.6	148.0	Potatoes	43.3	46.7
Chicken	41.8	52.9	Lettuce	20.9	23.5
Fish, shellfish	12.5	12.3	Tomatoes	10.3	11.8
Eggs	38.4	33.4	Onions	9.2	10.7
Dairy Products			**Fresh Fruit**		
Fluid milk	263.5	216.9	Bananas	18.0	22.6
Cheese	13.1	20.1	Apples	16.7	15.5
Ice cream	17.3	17.5	Oranges	14.1	12.3

Source: "Food Consumption, Prices, and Expenditures," U.S. Department of Agriculture, Economic Research Service

dressings and breaded fish fillets. One needs only to watch the commercials during any televised sporting event to realize that there is big competition between the brewers of "light" beers. Diet beverages now constitute an estimated 20 percent of the soft drink market.[8] There are even artificially sweetened diet cocoa mixes.

Other products are labeled "light" or "-free" to signal the removal of ingredients regarded by some consumers as health hazards. Campbell's light soups have reduced amounts of sodium. Produce canners seeking to bolster their sagging market share have introduced vegetables with less salt and fruits with less sugar. Caffeine-free soft drinks are now produced by all of the major manufacturers. Concern about preservatives has resulted in numerous "all natural" products — from potato chips to peanut butter to spaghetti sauces.

Contradictions in Consumption Statistics

It is hard to generalize about the effects of nutrition and diet concerns on grocery purchases. Among dairy products, the trend toward low-fat diets seems to be borne out. Per capita fluid milk and cream consumption fell from 264 pounds in 1972 to 228

[8] In 1982, the last year for which figures are available, the National Soft Drink Association said diet drinks comprised 17.7 percent of the total market.

pounds in 1980 to 217 pounds in 1982. Consumption of yogurt, a low-fat food favored by dieters and exercisers, soared from 0.25 pounds per person in 1962 to 2.71 pounds in 1982. Ice cream consumption stayed about the same in 1982 (17.5 pounds) as it was in 1972 (17.3 pounds) and was below the 1975 peak of 18.5 pounds. However, consumption of cheese, much of which is high in sodium as well as fat, jumped from 13.1 pounds in 1972 to 20.1 pounds in 1982, and the ice cream market was invaded by new "superpremium" brands, such as Haggen Dazs and Frusen Gladje, that contain more than 15 percent butterfat.

Cholesterol concern was a main, if not *the*, important factor in the decline in the consumption of eggs, down from 303 per capita in 1972 to 263 in 1982. But other statistics provide a mixed picture. Frozen vegetable consumption went up from 22.1 pounds in 1972 to 28.8 pounds in 1982; but most of that growth was in frozen french fries. Refined sugar consumption declined from 102.3 pounds per capita in 1972 to 75.2 pounds in 1982, but the use of corn sweeteners more than doubled from 21.1 to 48.2 pounds. Coffee consumption dropped by 27 percent, but soft drink consumption jumped by 56 percent.

Nutritionists and other advocates of low-fat, low-cholesterol diets are often accorded credit for the decline in red meat consumption and the rise in consumption of poultry and fish. Most media reports on diet and health trends note that Americans are eating less red meat. According to the U.S. Department of Agriculture, per capita beef consumption fell from 85.4 pounds in 1972 and 94.4 pounds in the peak year of 1976 to 77.3 pounds in 1982. Lamb and mutton consumption was down by almost half — 2.9 to 1.5 pounds. The 1982 per capita veal consumption — 1.6 pounds — was fairly even with the 1972 figure of 1.9 pounds, it was down from the 1975 peak of 3.4 pounds.

Sales of poultry jumped during the same period. Consumption of ready-to-cook chicken rose from 40.4 pounds per capita in 1970 to 52.9 pounds in 1982. Turkey, increasingly seen as more than a holiday food, went from 8.0 pounds per capita in 1970 to 10.8 in 1982. Chicken and turkey were marketed as a replacement for red meat in a number of products, such as chicken and turkey franks, and turkey "ham," pastrami and other cold cuts.

Representatives of the red meat industry protest that nutrition and diet are overrated as reasons for these changes. Tom McDermott, director of communications for the National Live Stock and Meat Board, said the decline in beef consumption is a result of the decline in beef supply, which in turn was caused by

Questions of Quality

Few complaints have been registered about the upsurge in fresh produce consumption, except perhaps among those in the frozen and canned produce industries. But there are complaints about the quality of the fruits and vegetables available to the average consumer.

Producers have developed hardy strains that can survive the rigors of weather, pests, packing and shipping but sometimes, it seems, at the cost of flavor. "If it's anything that grows, they [the big commercial growers] want it disease-resistant ... [they want] ease of picking, shippability, shelf life and all of that, and if flavor goes, well, you can't have everything," says food critic Mimi Sheraton.

The bugaboo of most food critics is the hothouse tomato, grown in an artificial environment and picked green, then sprayed with ethylene gas to give it a red appearance. These tomatoes never fully ripen and are usually pale orange rather than bright red in appearance.

This accounts, in part, for the popularity among serious cooks of produce specialty stores; in a survey by *The Packer* magazine, 8 percent of all respondents and 15 percent of respondents in the Northeast said they most frequently bought fresh produce from specialty stores.

Many of these shops are blessed with clients who are not only selective, but affluent: The tender loving care given these products raises their cost. For example, Dean & DeLuca in New York City recently carried California Driscoll Strawberries at $3.50 a pint and miniature summer squashes, a newly prized vegetable, at $7.50 a pound.

the economics of cattle raising. High profits in the early 1970s, McDermott said, led to overbreeding, which produced a market glut and lower profits. Massive livestock sales followed, causing a big increase in the supply of beef and in consumption during 1976-77. Since farmers and ranchers retained smaller herds, the supply has since become less plentiful.

"It is our contention that the industry has been affected more in the past five years from the economic conditions than it has by changes in lifestyle or taste or willingness to buy, although that has had an impact," McDermott said. To back up this contention, McDermott and others in the meat industry point to pork, which is less cyclical and has suffered less of a decline. While per capita consumption of pork — which was America's premier meat until passed by beef in the early 1950s — was less in 1982 (59.0 pounds) than in the peak year of 1980 (68.3 pounds), it was actually higher than it had been throughout much of the 1960s and 1970s.

Price also may have affected consumers' meat-buying decisions. Beef prices increased 138 percent between 1970 and 1982; pork prices went up 127 percent. But chicken prices increased only 76 percent during the period, and turkey prices increased 66 percent. Thus, the average prices of red meat ($2.43 a pound for beef, $1.75 a pound for pork in 1982) showed a greater disparity with those for poultry (72 cents a pound for broiler chickens, 93 cents a pound for turkeys). "The thing that probably saved the beef industry is that we are able to sell a lot of our product in ground form and that's the most price competitive form," McDermott said. Per capita consumption of hamburger showed a slight resurgence in the early 1980s, while more expensive cuts continued the steep decline that began in 1976.

Fast-Food Trends

THE OPTIMISM of beef producers could only have been bolstered by the popularity of the advertising campaign introduced by the Wendy's fast-food hamburger chain in January. In its television ads, a cantankerous but lovable elderly woman views what is presumably the competition's product — a tiny hamburger on a hyperbolically large bun — and shouts, "Where's the beef?" The slogan became an instant catchphrase; Democratic presidential contender Walter F. Mondale even used it to popularize his claim that opponent Gary Hart lacked substance.

Wendy's is not the only big chain to put its advertising emphasis on burgers. Burger King promotes its "broiled not fried" hamburgers, and recent advertisements have described industry leader McDonald's as "America's Meat and Potatoes." Meat industry officials view the development with satisfaction. "It does seem that there has been a reawakening on the part of some of the fast food industry that the biggest part of their business still comes from beef," McDermott said.

Hamburgers are big business in the United States. McDonald's, Burger King and Wendy's rank No. 1, 2 and 4 among franchised restaurant systems.[9] McDonald's, with 7,778 outlets and $8.6 billion in sales in 1983, remains king of fast food; its revenues were larger than the next three chains combined *(see box, p. 19)*.

---

[9] Kentucky Fried Chicken holds third place. Figures from "Franchising: Maturing Markets and Menus," *Restaurant Business*, March 20, 1984.

Richard and Maurice McDonald of San Bernardino, Calif., put up the first "golden arches" in 1948, but it was Ray Kroc who turned the concern into a fast-food empire. Kroc, who became franchising agent in 1953 and bought out the brothers in 1961, died last February at age 81. He is credited by many with having the foresight to exploit the demographic trends of increased mobility, more working mothers, busier lifestyles and growing numbers of single-person households.

A tribute published in *Nation's Restaurant News* said, "It is not an exaggeration to say Ray Kroc helped transform lifestyles — the very basic ritual of eating . . . Kroc has been compared to such pioneers as Henry Ford for the profound effect he has had on American life." Kroc reportedly had a net worth of $600 million when he died.

Diversification: A Key Word in Franchising

While burgers, fries and shakes formed the basis of the McDonald's empire, the company's executives have never rested on their buns. Their product line includes a fish sandwich and fried chicken "McNuggets." McDonald's also pioneered the fast-food breakfast, introducing its Egg McMuffin sandwich in 1973 and a full breakfast menu in 1977.

As competition has stiffened in the fast-food industry, diversification has become a central concern to company executives. This has become especially true as the baby-boom generation, the first to be born and raised in the fast-food era, has entered maturity. At a recent conference of fast-food executives, quality, "upscaling" and new menu items dominated the discussions. "It was obvious that all of them had studied the same demographic reports and concluded that their customers-of-choice for 1984 and beyond are the college-educated, weight-watching, upwardly mobile, fast food-weaned, health-conscious adults who were born in the boom years following World War II," Joe Edwards wrote in *Nation's Restaurant News*.[10]

Several fast-food chains, including Burger King, Wendy's and Roy Rogers, have installed salad bars in most of their restaurants. In 1983, Burger King introduced — or "rolled out," in industry jargon — salad sandwiches in pita bread. Hardee's, the fifth largest fast-food chain, offers a turkey club sandwich to go with its burgers and biscuit sandwiches.

Not all of the new products being offered are diet-oriented. Many are directed to the variety- and taste-consciousness of the target group. Wendy's now provides baked potatoes with a

---

[10] "Chain Leaders Target Strategies Toward Baby Boom Generation," *Nation's Restaurant News*, Jan. 2, 1984.

variety of cheese- or cream-sauce-based toppings. Jack in the Box, Arby's and Roy Rogers are marketing croissant sandwiches, although Roy Rogers, staying determinedly American, calls them "crescents." The Marriott-owned chain is also among those test-marketing all-you-can-eat breakfast buffets, featuring scrambled eggs, pancakes, bacon and sausages.

The interest in regional and ethnic food has sparked growth in several segments of the fast-food industry. Kentucky Fried Chicken continues its predominance among chicken franchisers, but "the Colonel" has found it necessary to roll out "fresh-from-scratch" buttermilk biscuits to counter competition from chains offering "authentic" Southern chicken and biscuits.

While Church's has a solid hold on second place with traditional chicken offerings, the fast-growing third- and fourth-place chains, Popeye's Famous Fried Chicken and Bojangle's Famous Chicken 'n' Biscuits, specialize in spicy "New Orleans style" chicken served with "Cajun" rice.[11] Other fried chicken chains evoke images of Southern home cooking: Grandy's Country Cookin', Mrs. Winner's Chicken and Biscuits, Sisters Chicken 'n' Biscuits.

PepsiCo, makers of Pepsi soft drinks, has made its mark in the pizza and Mexican fast-food areas; its Pizza Hut and Taco Bell chains are industry leaders. Deep-dish pizza is a hot item. Pizza Hut derives 75 percent of its sales from its "Pan Pizza" and the No. 2 chain, Godfather's Pizza, recently added deep-dish pizza to its lineup. "Gourmet" pizza franchisers are also growing, led by a Boston-based firm marketing the name of Pizzeria Uno, the Chicago restaurant that claims to have invented deep-dish pizza. However, Neapolitan pizza is not dead; Domino's Pizza, which specializes in home delivery of thin-crust pies, was one of last year's success stories, with sales growing 58 percent over 1982.

Upscaling Ice Cream and Chocolate Chips

Taco Bell, whose "Just Made for You" advertising echoes the "Have It Your Way" theme that made Burger King popular in the 1970s, is way out in front in the Mexican fast-food area. Its main competition appears to come not from other fast-food chains, but from the more "upscale" table-service Mexican food franchises. For example, Chi-Chi's leaped into the top 30 among franchise systems in 1983 with $198.5 million in sales, a 72 percent increase over 1982.

Enterprising restaurateurs are recognizing that bland,

---

[11] Bojangle's is owned by Horn and Hardart, a fast-food pioneer famous for its automats, the first of which opened in Philadelphia in 1902, followed by its more well-known New York outlets in 1912.

Top 15 Fast Food Franchises
(by sales in millions of dollars)

	1983 Sales	Outlets
1. McDonald's	$8,600	7,778
2. Burger King**	2,810	3,502
3. Kentucky Fried Chicken	2,623	6,609
4. Wendy's	1,800	2,671
5. Hardee's	1,718	2,154
6. Pizza Hut	1,671*	4,253
7. Dairy Queen**	1,288	4,751
8. Big Boy	1,000	1,230
9. Taco Bell	693*	1,663
10. Arby's	650	1,270
11. Church's	614*	1,446
12. Long John Silver's**	554.5	1,313
13. Ponderosa	554	682
14. Jack in the Box**	547	778
15. Dunkin' Donuts**	476	1,250

* Estimated by *Restaurant Business.*
** Figures based on fiscal year; rest based on calendar year.
Source: Restaurant Business.

standardized, styrofoam-wrapped food and plastic surroundings are the most common consumer complaints about fast-food restaurants. According to the National Restaurant Association's 1984 forecast, "Restaurant operators will be taking traditional fast-food concepts and repositioning them as upscale restaurants." "Gourmet" hamburger restaurants, featuring charcoal-broiled, half-pound burgers with a variety of toppings, are representative of this trend.

Upscale is also the word among dessert retailers. Longtime leaders Dairy Queen and Baskin Robbins still head the field, but "superpremium" ice creams are providing competition. Haggen Dazs, which opened its first store in 1970, now has over 300; Frusen Gladje has 50, mainly in New York, Baltimore and Dallas. Several chains, including Steve's in Boston (now nationally franchised) and Bob's in Washington, have turned a profit doing something most parents frown on if their own children do it: mixing ice cream, crushed cookies and candy bars.

Chocolate chip cookie stores are also the rage in many cities. In 1979, David Liederman of New York City opened his first David's Cookies store, offering an all-butter cookie with imported chocolate chunks. Despite an initial reluctance to franchise his concept because of quality-control concerns, Liederman now has 120 David's Cookies franchises, including one in Japan. "The cookie just caught the public's imagination," said William Liederman, David's brother and business partner. "He's just besieged by people that want a franchise."

The Liedermans are also gambling that people are ready for the ultimate food marriage of the 1980s: gourmet fast food. In July, they will open a restaurant in Manhattan called the Dine-o-Mat, which will serve small "sampler" portions of New American cuisine-style preparations. Diners will take plates of desired food from a conveyor belt, a gimmick borrowed from Japanese sushi bars. "I think that's a whole new direction this business is moving into," Liederman said. "Restaurants will be offering sampling menus and tasting things. People are less interested in getting a big hunk of something."

Selected Bibliography

Books

Hess, John L., and Karen Hess, *The Taste of America*, Grossman Publishers, 1977.
Hooker, Richard J., *Food and Drink in America*, Bobbs-Merrill, 1981.
Root, Waverley, and Richard de Rochemont, *Eating in America*, William Morrow & Co., 1976.

Articles

Claiborne, Craig, "Nouvelle Cuisine: Here To Stay," *The New York Times Magazine*, Dec. 18, 1983.
"Franchising: Maturing Menus and Markets," *Restaurant Business*, March 20, 1984.
"Fresh Attitudes," *The Packer*, May 1984.
Kanner, Bernice, "Cookie Dough," *New York*, April 9, 1984.
Nathan, Joan, and Elizabeth Sahatjian, "Whither the Great American Food Fad?" *Cuisine*, April 1984.
"New Study Shows Restaurant Distribution Across U.S.," *National Restaurant Association News*, September 1983.
Sheraton, Mimi, "Mesquite Comes to Town," *Time*, March 12, 1984.
Wallis, Claudia, "Hold The Eggs and Butter," *Time*, March 26, 1984.

Reports and Studies

"A Glowing Year Ahead," 1984 National Restaurant Association Forecast, December 1983.
"Annual Consumer Expenditures Study," *Supermarket Business*, September 1983.
Editorial Research Reports: "Fast Food: U.S. Growth Industry," 1978 Vol. II, p. 905; "Gourmet Cooking," 1971 Vol. I, p. 307.
"Meatfacts," American Meat Institute, 1983 edition.
"Nutrition & the American Restaurant," Public Voice for Food and Health Policy, September 1983.

Graphics: Cover illustration, other graphics by Staff Artist Belle Burkhart.

COUNTRY

MUSIC

by

Marc Leepson

May 31
1 9 8 5

COUNTRY MUSIC

I T IS POSSIBLE for a visitor to Nashville not to fall under the spell of the country music scene. But it is not likely. After all, this is a city where the professional baseball team is called the Sounds, the signs in the airport welcome tourists to "Music City, U.S.A." and the featured attraction is the venerable country music institution, the Grand Ole Opry. The country music business pumps about $1 billion a year into Nashville's economy. At last count, 22 record companies had offices in town. Nashville also has 42 country music recording studios, 60 record producers, 25 independent record promoters, 33 country talent agencies, more than 300 country music publishers, and 19 public relations agencies — not to mention several thousand country musicians and songwriters.[1]

A visitor staying at the Hall of Fame Motor Inn or Shoney's Inn can be jarred out of bed at nine o'clock on a Sunday morning by country tunes blaring from speakers outside the Country Music Outlet, a retail store that sells albums, tapes and souvenirs at "factory-to-you prices." The two motels stand on the edge of Music Row, a three-block square section on the downtown side of the Cumberland River. Music Row is home to most of Nashville's record companies, studios, producers, promoters and talent agencies and attracts thousands of songwriters and musicians looking for their big break. Music Row also features a string of tourist-attracting country music record and souvenir stores owned by big stars like Loretta Lynn, Hank Williams Jr., Barbara Mandrell, Alabama and Conway Twitty.

The premier country music radio station in Nashville is WSM, one of only 11 clear-channel, 50,000-watt AM stations in the nation. WSM not only broadcasts the Opry to much of the South on Friday and Saturday nights, but also has a six-piece studio band playing country tunes on the "Waking Crew," the station's long-running weekday morning program. It's a fair bet that no other local television station in the nation can match WSMV-TV's daily output of live country music. Each weekday

---

[1] Figures compiled by the Country Music Association, an 8,000-member trade organization of the country music industry.

the Nashville station airs two country music shows, each with a live studio band. The Nashville Network, the country cable channel that began operations in March 1983, currently sends 18 hours of "country and Western entertainment" each day to some 21.2 million households nationwide.[2]

Nashville is the center of a unique genre of American popular music that evolved from Anglo-Irish folk melodies first played more than two centuries ago by settlers in the Appalachian Mountains and other back-country areas of the South. Referred to as "hillbilly" music during the 1920s, when it first claimed widespread audiences, it then evolved into what was known after World War II as "country and Western" music. Today this hybrid and still-changing art form is simply called country music.

Country music "deals in simplicity that roots itself in reality, that speaks of love, grief and other basic emotions with frankness," author Robert Shelton said. It "is unashamed of being sentimental and nostalgic [and] places sincerity higher on its ladder of values than refinement."[3] Writer Paul Hemphill has called it the "soul music of the white South."[4]

Grand Ole Opry: An Enduring Attraction

WSM is the main reason that Nashville became the home of country music. The pivotal event came 60 years ago, on Nov. 28, 1925, when Uncle Jimmy Thompson, an 80-year-old fiddle player, stepped in front of a microphone in WSM's downtown studio and spun out an hour's worth of old-time country tunes. That was the first broadcast of the WSM Barn Dance, which two years later was christened the Grand Ole Opry.[5] By the late 1940s the Opry was the showcase of country music. Most of the Opry's stars moved to Nashville, and the music's commercial segment soon followed. "As the singers moved in, so did the musical entrepreneurs — the booking agents, the artist and repertory men, the promoters," Tulane University historian Bill C. Malone noted. "With the evident emergence of Nashville as the ranking country-music center, the commercial fraternity flocked there to be near the performers." By 1957, Malone said,

---

[2] The Nashville Network, WSM Radio and the Grand Ole Opry are owned and operated by Dallas-based Gaylord Broadcasting Co., which also owns Opryland, the theme park in which the Grand Ole Opry has been performed since 1974. The Opry was first staged in a WSM studio. It then had temporary homes in a movie theater and Nashville's War Memorial Auditorium before moving to the Ryman Auditorium in 1943, where it stayed until its 1974 move to the new Opry House. WSMV-TV is owned by Gillett Broadcasting Co. of Nashville.

[3] Robert Shelton, *The Country Music Story*, (1966), p. 11

[4] Paul Hemphill, *The Nashville Sound*, (1970), p. 12.

[5] George D. Hay, the show's original announcer, thought up the name on the air one night in 1927, two years after the WSM Barn Dance had begun. According to the official *Opry Picture-History Book*, following the broadcast of an opera show, Hay said, "For the past hour we have been listening to music taken largely from Grand Opera, but from now on we will present 'The Grand Ole Opry.'" The Saturday night Opry radio show is the longest-running continuously broadcast program in the history of the medium.

The Opry House outside Nashville, home of the Grand Ole Opry (bottom inset), a phrase coined by radio announcer George D. Hay in 1927 (top inset).

Nashville "had come to rival New York and Hollywood as a recording center." [6]

The Grand Ole Opry today is vastly different from the folksy hour of fiddle tunes that inaugurated it. Each show has dozens of performers.[7] Some play music that was popular half a century ago; others do renditions of the latest Nashville sounds. Opry performance No. 3,093, on April 13, for example, opened with Roy Acuff, the 81-year-old "King of Country Music," singing "Wabash Cannon Ball," which he first recorded in 1936. Later in the evening Charlie Walker, an Opry regular for 18 years, did a rendition of "The San Antonio Rose," the Western swing theme song of Bob Wills that was initially recorded in 1938 and three years later was a big hit for Bing Crosby.

That same show included a comedy routine by Minnie Pearl, who has been telling corny jokes on the Opry stage for more than 30 years. Bill Monroe, who first played the Opry in 1939, and his Bluegrass Boys performed as did the Stanley Brothers. Miniskirted Lorrie Morgan crooned Willie Nelson's pop-coun-

---

[6] Bill C. Malone, *Country Music U.S.A.* (1968), pp. 214, 252. Malone's book, which was based on his doctoral dissertation from the University of Texas, is widely regarded as the most thoroughly researched history of country music. An updated, revised edition is scheduled to be published this year.

[7] There is one performance of the Opry every Friday night, two every Saturday evening. Additional shows are added during the tourist season from late spring to early fall.

try hit "Crazy" backed by her band of young, long-haired musicians who looked and sounded very much like rock 'n' roll performers. The flashy clothes and smooth sounds of The Four Guys, a vocal quartet, would have been at home in a Las Vegas lounge. Resplendent in their brightly colored, spangled suits were Hank Snow, an Opry regular for 35 years, and Porter Wagoner, backed up by his all-female band.

The April 13 Opry performance was sold out; tickets need to be ordered well in advance to ensure a good seat at the 4,400-seat Opry House. Full houses are but one indication of country music's widespread popularity. Other signs include the unexpectedly quick success of the Nashville Network, which on April 13 aired the first of its weekly live telecasts of the Opry. The country cable network grew faster than any other cable channel during its first year of operation and now is available in more than 25 percent of the nation's households with television. Many country acts are drawing large numbers of paying customers at concerts around the country. The band Alabama, for example, one of the most popular country acts, is selling out virtually all its concerts on its current tour. According to the Country Music Association (CMA), reigning country superstar Kenny Rogers had the second-highest grossing concert tour in show business last year, behind rock star Michael Jackson but ahead of Bruce Springsteen and Billy Joel.

The wide popularity of the 1980 movie "Urban Cowboy," a film that glamorized the country-music lifestyle, helped bring about booming record sales and brought new audiences to country music radio stations during the early 1980s. The number of full-time country radio stations increased from 1,534 in 1980 to 2,114 two years later. A 1984 CMA survey found that 3,138 radio stations play country music in the United States and Canada and 2,265 stations program country music full time.

Worrisome Falloff in Ratings, Record Sales

But there are some clouds in the country music business picture. For one thing, the number of full-time country music stations declined slightly in 1984 following 11 years of steady growth. And ratings were down last year. According to figures compiled by Arbitron, the ratings service, last fall country radio stations in the nation's top 50 markets attracted 9.9 percent of all listeners aged 12 and above, compared with 11.8 percent two years earlier.[8] Ratings seem to have picked up in some markets late in 1984 and early this year, restoring optimism in some quarters about country radio's financial future.

"How successful [country] radio stations are depends on your

---

[8] See *Closeup*, the official monthly publication of the Country Music Association, May 1985, pp. 1, 3-4.

perspective," said Ed Salamon, the head of programming for United Stations Radio Network, which provides news and music shows to some 700 country music stations. "Country radio has declined in the last couple of years as compared with the 'Urban Cowboy'-influenced bump or bubble [of the early 1980s]. It has not declined compared to what country radio was in the pre-'Urban Cowboy' days. It's grown.... A lot of us feel that country is very healthy and getting healthier." [9]

Country music radio has changed significantly during the last 15 years, widening its audiences in Northern cities such as New York and Chicago. "There was a change in the presentation of country radio from people that sounded like rural, 'howdy folks' announcers to a presentation that people who lived in cities could get into," Salamon said. The smoother-sounding country announcers added songs from country-flavored rock stars such as Linda Ronstadt and the Eagles. At the same time, play lists began to narrow. Today, many full-time country stations play fewer than 40 different current records in a given broadcast day.

Programmers praise the format, but some record company officials have expressed concerns about it. "What they're doing is what killed Top 40 radio a few years back — tightening up, playing fewer records, repetition, repetition," a country recording industry executive said. "The adult consumer will stand for less of that than the kids [who listened to Top 40] did. And even the kids got tired of it," he said, noting that a large segment of the country music audience is over 25. "It's going to backfire in their face a lot faster." Bill Sherard, president and general manager of WPKX-FM, a country music station in Washington, D.C., disagreed. Country music "is still the only format with a hometown," he said. "Since it's based on what I would call traditional [musical] chord structures and white man's soul — generally story music and melodies and words that people can comprehend and learn easily — it'll always have a place in the musical format...."

The recording end of the country music business also has felt a post-"Urban Cowboy" slump. In 1981, eight country albums each sold more than a million copies and 31 albums each accounted for more than $1 million in sales, according to figures compiled by the Recording Industry Association of America (RIAA). Last year only five country albums sold more than a million copies and only 13 earned more than $1 million. RIAA surveys also indicate steady annual decreases since 1981 in country music's percentage of all retail and record club sales. In 1983, the last year for which complete statistics are available,

---

[9] Salamon and others quoted in this report were interviewed by the author, unless otherwise indicated.

country records accounted for 13 percent of all dollars spent in retail record stores — down from 15 percent in 1981. In 1983 country represented 20 percent of all records and tapes sold by mail, compared with 24 percent in both 1981 and 1982.

Nick Hunter, senior vice president for sales and promotion at Warner Brothers Records in Nashville, mentioned singer Ray Price, one of the most popular country performers in the late 1950s and early 1960s, when asked about the recent sag in record sales. "In the early sixties someone asked Ray Price why he added strings and went for more of a pop sound in country music," Hunter said. "Price said, 'Back then, a successful country record sale was considered 100,000 and I thought I could do better by changing my sound.' Today, in 1985, a successful country record is still considered 100,000. We haven't grown that much."

Record sales may be declining because listeners first attracted to country by "Urban Cowboy" are losing interest. Another factor is that fewer country acts are selling records to non-country audiences — the so-called "crossover" market. During the early 1980s Dolly Parton, Willie Nelson, Mac Davis, Kenny Rogers, Anne Murray and a few other country performers had million sellers on the country, pop and rock music charts. But in 1984 the crossover cupboard was bare. At this year's Grammy Awards, for example, no country music records were nominated for record of the year, album of the year or song of the year. In recent years country performers routinely received nominations in those categories.

A third reason is the competition for record dollars from the revitalized pop and rock music scene. In the early 1980s "pop music was dead," said Al Cooley, general manager of Combine Music, a Nashville country music publisher. "So people were getting turned on to [country acts such as] Willie Nelson, Waylon Jennings, Kenny Rogers and Dolly Parton. They were buying records by the millions." But today, Cooley said, "pop music is really happening."

Another crucial factor influencing record sales is the "graying" of the country music audience. Demographic surveys indicate that country music fans are significantly older than the average record buyer. A survey done by CBS Records found that today's average country music listener is 38-39 years old, compared with an average age of 31-32 in 1979. An RIAA survey found that 75 percent of all country music record buyers are 25 or older. "The aging process results in fewer country albums being sold, as older adults drop out of the active record buying public," the editors of *Closeup,* a CMA publication, reported in the May 1985 issue. Hunter put it more succinctly: "We're appealing to an audience that's now basically over 40," he said, "and they don't buy records."

Industry officials say that sales have picked up in 1985, and many are optimistic about the future. They say that new country artists are beginning to appeal to younger audiences and that the growing popularity of music containing traditional influences *(see p. 35)* will attract older fans. "There may have been a down trend, but I think that now we're back on the increase again," said Cathleen Gurley, CMA's public information director.

Evolving Musical Form

TODAY'S COUNTRY MUSIC is a blend of musical and cultural influences whose roots were the folk songs brought into this country by the earliest settlers from England, Scotland, Wales and Ireland. Country music, historian Malone wrote, "developed out of a reservoir of folksongs and ballads brought to North America by the Anglo-Celtic immigrants and gradually absorbed influences from other musical sources until it emerged as a force strong enough to survive, and even thrive, in an urban-industrial-oriented society." [10] Chief among the "other musical sources" were blues music performed by Southern blacks, religious music of Southern churches and different forms of 19th- and early 20th-century popular music, including songs from Tin Pan Alley, vaudeville and medicine shows.

Although Anglo-Irish folk tunes and ballads were carried into every other section of the country, only in the South did conditions prove ripe for the development of an original American musical form, what Malone termed "a lasting regional music." "This happened," Robert Shelton wrote, "partially because of a complex of conservative factors in the primarily agrarian economy of the South. Partly, too, it stemmed from the strong hold of frontier religious institutions, which included music." [11]

Gradually Americans began to fit American themes to the Old World music. The Irish lament, "Let My Soul Pass Through Ireland" became "Let My Soul Pass Through the Southland." Another example is the "Half Crown Song." "In the English-Irish version," said American vernacular music expert Richard Spottswood, "a guy goes into a restaurant with a very hungry

[10] Malone, *op cit.*, p. 3.
[11] Shelton, *op. cit.*, p. 25.

woman and he only has half a crown to pay for this gigantic meal. The American version is called 'I Just Had Fifty Cents.' "

For the most part the early Southern white folk songs were sung without musical accompaniment, usually by one person in a high-pitched, nasal voice.[12] The first instruments that made their way into the rural areas were the dulcimer and the fiddle. Slaves introduced the banjo, which was derived from an African instrument called the *bania*. The banjo became popular among white rural musicians in the latter decades of the 19th century, about the same time that the guitar and mandolin came on the scene. The instruments, of course, influenced the way the music was sung. The crude, high-pitched voices began to give way to more melodic singing. Group harmony, which had been around long before the popularity of musical instruments, adapted well into the new instrumental blend.

Radio, Records Expand Audience in 1920s

Until the early 1920s the folk music of the white rural South was not widely known in the rest of the country. Then the invention of the phonograph record markedly changed both the nature of the music and its audience. The first commercial country music recording was made by two old-time fiddlers, Eck Robertson from Texas and Henry Gilliland from Virginia. The date was June 1922 — a year after the introduction of the phonograph record. "They went up to New York City on kind of a lark to make some records," said Bill McNeil, a folklorist with the Ozark Folk Center in Mountain View, Ark. "They recorded 'Arkansas Traveler' and 'Sally Goodin.' That generally is cited as the first commercial recording by a country musician that was slanted toward a country audience and is considered the beginning of the commercial country music industry." Fiddlin' John Carson, a popular radio musician, recorded the first hit country music record in Atlanta on June 14, 1923. When Carson's "The Old Hen Cackled" started selling, he signed a contract with Okeh Records, becoming the first country music performer to have his records marketed commercially.

After Carson's success, record companies "rushed into the South and Southwest with their field units," Malone commented, "recording almost indiscriminately any country musicians they could find."[13] Ralph Peer, Okeh's recording director who also was a pioneering folklore collector of both black and white Southern music, was responsible for tagging this genre "hillbilly music." The term had been in use since the turn of the century to describe backwoods Southerners.[14] Its new

[12] For background, see Alan Lomax, *The Folk Songs of North America* (1960), p. 153.
[13] Malone, *op. cit.*, p. 42.
[14] For background, see Archie Green, "Hillbilly Music: Source and Symbol," *Journal of American Folklore*, July-September 1965, pp. 204-228.

Three of the most influential performers in country music history: *from left,*
Bob Wills, Hank Williams and Jimmie Rodgers

application occurred when Peer decided to call a then-unnamed
band the Hillbillies after the group made its first record on Jan.
15, 1925.

Peer was the first to record many musicians, including the
two most successful hillbilly acts of the 1930s — Jimmie Rodgers and the Carter Family. He discovered both in August 1927
at a series of audition sessions held in Bristol on the Tennessee-
Virginia border. The Carter Family — A.P., his wife Sara and
his sister-in-law Maybelle — from Maces Spring, Va., made
more than 150 records and were one of the most popular country music groups in the country for decades. Their simple,
church-influenced songs and their style of musicianship influenced generations of country and folk musicians.

Rodgers, a former railroad brakeman from Meridian, Miss.,
hit it big in the late 1920s with his pining, yodeling songs of
hard work and hard times. Rodgers, who is regarded as the
father of modern country music and was the first country singing star, died of tuberculosis in 1933. His songs, heavily influenced by black country-blues singers, had a profound impact
on country music. "Rodgers had demonstrated that a country
boy, singing about his kind of life, could fall into the big money
and adulation if he merely learned a few tricks," Paul Hemphill
wrote. "From the day Rodgers died, then, they started coming
out of the woods: country boys, many of them trying to emulate
Rodgers' blue yodels, seeking out recording executives and
straining for the brass ring." [15]

Country music owed a large measure of its increasing popularity to another new 1920s electronic medium: radio. Country acts
began playing in front of radio microphones at stations such as
WSB in Atlanta and WBAP in Fort Worth, Texas, in 1922 —

[15] Hemphill, *op. cit.,* p. 134.

two years after Pittsburgh's KDKA, the first commercial broadcasting station, went on the air. About a week after it began broadcasting in April 1924, Chicago's WLS began a weekly show of hillbilly music that later was called the National Barn Dance. It was the most popular hillbilly music show in the nation for many years. Cowboy singer Gene Autry from Tioga, Texas, was a featured attraction on the National Barn Dance in the early 1930s. In 1934 the WLS show was broadcast nationally on the NBC radio network. The Grand Ole Opry, which began in November 1925 as the WSM Barn Dance in Nashville, rivaled the National Barn Dance in popularity by the late 1930s.

Western Style Influential in 1930s and '40s

Country music's popularity spread rapidly during the 1930s. Dozens of radio stations in the South and Midwest popularized the music in those areas of the country. Illegal radio stations beaming powerful signals from just inside the Mexican border sent hillbilly music throughout most of the rest of the United States. It was during the 1930s, too, that Western music, primarily from Texas and Oklahoma, began to influence the Southern white musical scene. Thomas F. Johnson of Texas A&M University defines Western music as "the trans-Mississippi, folk-based popular music of ... groups such as trappers, miners, loggers, drifters and nomadic herders (cowboys), who occupied the American West before the coming of agricultural settlers." Western music, Johnson said, deals with an "image of the free, unfettered individual," characterized by "the image of the cowboy and his herd of dogies." It is music that celebrates "the wilderness as existentially, morally, and spiritually good and restorative...." [16]

The Western music of the 1930s was diverse. Southwestern bands attired in Western clothing with names such as The Riders of the Purple Sage, the Sons of the Pioneers and the Girls of the Golden West, sang of lonesome nights on the range. Singing cowboys such as Gene Autry, Ken Maynard, Roy Rogers (an original member of the Sons of the Pioneers) and Tex Ritter crooned their way through scores of Western movies. Hard-driving honky-tonk singers such as Ernest Tubb belted out songs in a milieu of dim lights, thick smoke and loud music.

And there was Western swing, a hybrid music blending elements of country, pop, blues and jazz. Western swing bands played up-tempo dance tunes and featured clarinets, saxophones, trumpets and drums as well as fiddles, basses and steel guitars. The genre's foremost exponent was Bob Wills, a fiddler from West Texas who formed a band called the Texas Playboys

---

[16] Thomas F. Johnson, "That Ain't Country: The Distinctiveness of Commercial Western Music," *JEMF Quarterly*, summer 1981, p. 75.

Longtime Opry regulars: *from left,* Minnie Pearl and Roy Acuff, Bill Monroe of bluegrass fame and Eddy Arnold, the "Tennessee Plowboy."

in the early 1930s. Wills' brand of Western swing had a powerful impact on country music, especially in the early- and mid-1940s. "Western swing was just about the only kind of music you could hear in the state of Texas [in the 1940s]," said country music star Willie Nelson, who was born in Fort Worth and raised in Abbott, Texas. "Until Hank Williams came along, it was just Bob Wills. He was *it.* . . . Everyone listened to the Grand Ole Opry on Saturday nights, but the Nashville music never was as popular as Western swing in Texas." [17]

After World War II the music became known as country and Western music, or C&W, reflecting the enormous impact that Western music had during the previous 15 years. The commercially popular C&W music of the postwar era bore little resemblance to the string band music of the 1920s as its purveyors tried to erase the hillbilly image. C&W was a new, "nationalized country music," says folklorist and country music authority Archie Green. The industry, he said, "used phrases like 'getting rid of the hay bales and the hicks.' . . . Clearly, 'hillbilly' was too pejorative, backwoodsy, rural, L'il Abner." [18]

The country music industry that evolved was anything but backwoods. C&W stars got rich through big record sales and sold-out concerts around the nation. A group of Grand Ole Opry performers including Ernest Tubb played Carnegie Hall in New York City in October 1947 — the first time country musicians ever graced that august stage. The Opry drew country talent from across the country. The first big C&W star of the postwar

---

[17] Writing in *Country Music Magazine,* July-August 1984.
[18] Green, the author of *Only A Miner: Studies in Recorded Coal-Mining Songs* (1972), is a retired professor of folklore from the University of Texas.

era was Eddy Arnold, who called himself "The Tennessee Plowboy." Arnold's smooth singing style sold millions of records in the late 1940s. Among the other popular C&W performers of the period were Lefty Frizzell of Corsica, Texas, and a Canadian, Clarence E. "Hank" Snow.

The biggest star of the era, though, was Hank Williams. After recording an old country-blues tune called "Lovesick Blues" in 1949, Williams' career took off like the proverbial rocket. In the next four years he recorded 11 million-sellers. "Williams, lanky and hungry and possessing more white soul than any one man should be allowed to have, took a half-dozen encores the first time he sang ['Lovesick Blues'] at the Opry and the record fixed things so he would never again have to worry about money," Hemphill said. "He began grossing $200,000 a year, and he was one of the biggest names in *any* branch of music." [19] Williams, who was beset with personal and physical problems, died of a heart attack on New Year's Day 1953 at the peak of his celebrity. He was not yet 30 years old.[20]

From Rock 'n' Roll to the Nashville Sound

Hank Williams' death coincided with the birth of rock 'n' roll. This new music was essentially a fusion of white and black soul music, of C&W and rhythm and blues.[21] Its loud, throbbing beat became the anthem of the nation's teenagers within a year after Williams' death. In 1955 Elvis Presley, a 20-year-old from Tupelo, Miss., began churning out rock 'n' roll hits, eclipsing Williams' fame, fortune and influence. Elvis popularized a type of country-influenced rock 'n' roll called "rockabilly" that sprang up in Memphis in the early 1950s. One critic described it as "a fast, aggressive music: simple, snappy drumming, sharp guitar licks, wild country boogie piano, the music of [white] kids who came from all over the South." [22] Among the other rockabilly pioneers were future country stars Jerry Lee Lewis from Ferriday, La., and Arkansas native Johnny Cash.

During rock 'n' roll's heyday in the late 1950s many country musicians continued playing as they always had. But others embraced elements of the new music. "Although some country performers prospered because of their willingness to compromise, for a period pure country music suffered, and, to many tradition-minded fans, the old music seemed on its way to destruction," Malone noted.[23] The old music, of course, was not destroyed. Country music instead evolved by the early 1960s

---

[19] Hemphill, *op. cit.*, pp. 155-156.
[20] Williams was born on Sept. 17, 1923, in Mt. Olive, Ala.
[21] See section of the development of rock 'n' roll in "Rock Music Business," *E.R.R.* 1977 Vol. I, pp. 433-452.
[22] Greil Marcus, *Mystery Train* (1975), pp. 164-65.
[23] Malone, *op. cit.*, pp. 245-246.

into a sound that retained its country roots. The music was developed in Nashville recording studios primarily by guitarist-producer Chet Atkins, the head of RCA Victor's Nashville branch, and independent producer Owen Bradley. Called country-pop or countrypolitan by some, the music is more widely known as the Nashville Sound.

"The Nashville Sound is a specific combination of musical elements and recording techniques that came together in the early sixties as country music was inventing a response to rock 'n' roll," said Bill Ivey, director of the Country Music Foundation in Nashville.[24] The new sound, which held sway for the next decade, contained string and horn sections, leaned heavily on rhythm guitars and typically used pop-style background singers. "It was developed in a team atmosphere," Ivey said. "Basically the same session musicians played on virtually every hit record."

Some have criticized the Nashville Sound as soulless, homogenized music that pandered to popular taste and wandered too far from its roots. "The texts became bland on the whole and non-controversial and the music became even blander than it had been under C&W," Archie Green said. Some Nashville musicians reacted against the strictures of the Nashville Sound. A small group, most notably Willie Nelson, left the city in the early 1970s and recorded successful records in Texas. Although the performers never put a name to it, the Texas country music of the early 1970s came to be called "outlaw" music. And it continues to have an influence. "You can look at the so-called 'outlaw' movement," Ivey said, "as presenting an alternative to the Nashville Sound, a way of getting back to basics."

Returning to Tradition

OLD-TIME OR TRADITIONAL country music has not faded away entirely, but for the most part it has survived outside the commercial sphere. "When we speak about old-time country music, as opposed to modern [commercial] country music, it's closer to a folk music," said McNeil of the Ozark Folk Center. Traditional, old-style country music still is performed

---

[24] The Country Music Foundation is a non-profit organization that works to preserve the heritage of country music. The foundation, located in Nashville, runs the Country Music Hall of Fame and Museum as well as a library and various research facilities.

regularly, but not in giant indoor sports arenas, and it is not recorded by major companies. Traditional music is performed at folk centers such as McNeil's, at festivals and church-basement-type concerts. It is recorded on small labels and played at odd hours on radio stations in some areas of the country. Very few musicians make their living as traditional country music performers.

One type of old-time country music — bluegrass — however, retains a significant following. Bluegrass music dates only from 1945 when country musician Bill Monroe put together a band called the Blue Grass Boys. The band consisted of Monroe on mandolin, along with a banjo player, fiddler, acoustic guitarist and stand-up bass. The music was up-tempo; the singing high-pitched mountain style. Although similar music had been played before, Monroe and his Blue Grass Boys are universally credited with the "birth" of bluegrass. "That's when bluegrass matured," music expert Spottswood said. "It became essentially a five-piece band playing music that was under the direction and inspiration of one man and evolved into the form that we know it today."

Many believe that the banjo is the pivotal instrument in bluegrass. The banjo "is the only instrument that you could not leave out and still say you have a bluegrass band," said Jerry Gray, a bluegrass and country music disc jockey at WAMU-FM in Washington. "You could do without a fiddle and maybe have a mandolin instead. You could do without a mandolin and have a dobro instead. You could do without a dobro and have a fiddle instead. But you have to have a banjo. That's what makes it a bluegrass band."

The originator of the standard bluegrass banjo technique is Earl Scruggs, a North Carolinian who joined Monroe's band shortly after it was formed. Scruggs was the first five-string banjoist to play lead, rather than strum the rhythm. "Scruggs style" banjo picking has been the norm in bluegrass ever since.[25]

Bluegrass music won new listeners during the urban folk revival of the early 1960s. Its popularity has since waned in New York and Chicago, but bluegrass still has a strong following throughout the Middle Atlantic states and in other regions of the country. In the Washington, D.C., area, for example, local clubs regularly present bluegrass bands and one public radio station runs six hours of bluegrass music every day. Many bluegrass musicians are able to make a living playing at large weekend bluegrass festivals held throughout the country.

[25] Scruggs and guitarist Lester Flatt put together their own bluegrass band in 1948. Scruggs' "Foggy Mountain Breakdown" probably is the most popular bluegrass composition ever written. For background see L. Mayne Smith, "An Introduction to Bluegrass," *Journal of American Folklore*, July-September 1965, p. 246.

Earl Scruggs *(top right)*, originator of "Scruggs-style" banjo-picking, flanked by new traditionalists Emmylou Harris *(left)* and Ricky Skaggs *(bottom right)*.

Is bluegrass, which took its present form just 40 years ago, genuine traditional music? Spottswood characterized it as "a derivative of modern country music that has chosen to keep one eye more or less on the roots in a particular way." Gray, on the other hand, said that bluegrass is an authentic type of traditional country music. "Charlie Waller of [the influential bluegrass band] the Country Gentlemen thinks it's the only real country music being played today," Gray said, "because it's acoustic and it's what real country mountain people played on their back porches years ago."

Gray divides bluegrass music into three categories: traditional, middle of the road and progressive. Traditional bluegrass is the type played by Bill Monroe, the Stanley Brothers and other bands that stick with old-time songs and unamplified instruments. Middle of the road, Gray said, is the brand of music played by bands such as the Country Gentlemen and Seldom Scene in which the old form is used but newer songs, including folk, rock and country tunes, are incorporated. "They've brought a lot of people in and kind of bridge the gap between the old and new," Gray said. Progressive groups such as the Dillards and the New Grass Revival play traditional bluegrass melodies but experiment with electrified instruments and drums.

Gray says it is unlikely that bluegrass will emulate Nashville and become influenced heavily by pop music. "I don't think there's much danger of it in the sense that bluegrass music will never be a music that is real popular or get much radio exposure. . . . I don't think there'll ever be enough money in it to worry about it."

There is a great deal of money, of course, to be made in Nashville. Most of the top moneymakers are performers who have infused country music with pop-oriented styles. Singer-songwriter Dolly Parton's most recent hits, for example, have been pop-style duets with Kenny Rogers. Parton also appears in big-production Las Vegas performances and has written the music for three motion pictures in which she has starred. Another example is the popular group Alabama. In the last few years this four-member band has sold more records than any other country music group. Alabama's last five albums all have gone "multi-platinum" — record company parlance for selling more than two million copies. The band has had 15 consecutive No. 1 singles on the country charts and has reaped numerous honors from the industry.

Alabama's pop-country sound obviously goes over well with audiences, but the band has not received a great deal of critical acclaim. "To their detractors," critic Joe Sasfy wrote recently, "Alabama plays redneck bubblegum music, an expertly crafted simile of real C&W designed to corral the youth audience." As for the group's latest album, Sasfy joined the detractors' chorus, saying the record is filled with "mawkish balladry that simply highlights the group's lack of distinctive vocal personality." [26]

Sasfy's criticism, however, pales in comparison with the words Archie Green used to describe the music of Kenny Rogers, country's most popular performer. "In terms of [earning] money, he's No. 1. In terms of esthetics and in terms of values he's way at the bottom," Green said. "Kenny in a sense represents the kind of stars that will be produced if we move into an Orwellian high-tech society: homogenized, bland, gutless."

Breaking Away from Pop-Style Commercialism

In recent years a small wave of country musicians has moved away from the pop influence and worked traditional elements into their music. The group includes John Anderson, Moe Bandy, the Judds, Merle Haggard, Emmylou Harris, Reba McEntire, Willie Nelson, Ricky Skaggs, George Strait, the Whites, Keith Whitley and Hank Williams Jr. Some, especially Willie Nelson, have succeeded commercially; virtually all have received lavish praise from critics. "In 1962-63-64 the creative cutting edge in Nashville was in the Nashville Sound; today I'd say the creative cutting edge is in the work of people I would characterize as more traditionalist," said Ivey of the Country Music Foundation. These musicians, Ivey said, "are performing in either old-time or hard-core mainstream country styles — styles that don't imitate, but emulate the styles that were cur-

---

[26] Writing in *The Washington Post*, April 12, 1985.

rent before the Nashville Sound, like Hank Williams, honky-tonk or bluegrass styles of things around the '40s and '50s."

Of these new traditionalists, 31-year-old Ricky Skaggs of Cordell, Ky., has received the lion's share of critical acclaim. Writing in *The New York Times* Feb. 25, 1985, critic Stephen Holden called Skaggs "the most commanding figure of a movement within country music to restore traditional values to a genre increasingly dominated by Hollywood production values and songwriting styles." Skaggs sings, writes his own material, plays guitar, banjo, mandolin and fiddle and produces a bluegrass-tinged brand of country music. Skaggs lists bluegrass, country and rock as his main musical influences.

The new traditionalists who are making their mark on the country music scene are not abandoning Nashville. Most of them live and work there. Some former rock musicians have moved to Nashville recently to try their hand at country. Country music singer Emmylou Harris, who had been turning out hit albums for a decade from her home in Los Angeles, also recently moved to Nashville. In the past, Harris had made bluegrass- and rock 'n' roll-influenced albums, and her move to Nashville is in part attributable to her interest in traditional and honky-tonk country music. "When country music got more and more homogenized a few years ago, I got very pessimistic," Harris has said. "Now I'm very optimistic again...." [27]

Despite the new attention being paid to traditionalists, it is unlikely that they will dominate commercial country music. Archie Green describes performers who "respect old-time material" as "conscious resistors" against the pull of Nashville's commercialism. "Nashville is really Tin Pan Gulch — an extension of Broadway in that sense," Green said. "It imposes its hegemony on country musicians, Appalachian musicians, rural musicians. Only a few counter it in some conscious way.... But if a Ricky Skaggs or a Willie Nelson achieves popularity, I don't think it changes Nashville, but it makes the moguls sit up. And what they usually do is then absorb it." Green predicted that Nashville will "stay as a center of a worldwide 'countrypolitan,' or country-pop music. It absorbs. It absorbed the 'outlaws.' It absorbs and tames...." Hunter of Warner Brothers Records agreed. "You're going to see a melting pot of musical things coming in and being called country. I think country will actually sound different and be a little different, but it'll still be country."

---

[27] Quoted in *The Washington Post*, March 27, 1985.

Selected Bibliography

Books

Artis, Bob, *Bluegrass,* Hawthorn, 1975.

Cornfield, Robert, *Just Country,* McGraw-Hill, 1976.

Green, Archie, *Only A Miner: Studies in Recorded Coal-Mining Songs,* University of Illinois Press, 1972.

Green, Douglas, *Country Roots,* Hawthorn, 1976.

Hemphill, Paul, *The Nashville Sound: Bright Lights and Country Music,* Simon & Schuster, 1970.

Malone, Bill C., *Country Music, U.S.A.: A Fifty Year History,* University of Texas Press, 1968.

——, *Southern Music, American Music,* University Press of Kentucky, 1979.

Shelton, Robert, *The Country Music Story,* Bobbs-Merrill, 1966.

Stambler, Irwin, and Grelun Landon, *The Encyclopedia of Folk, Country and Western Music,* St. Martin's Press, 1983.

Strobel, Jerry, ed., *Official Opry Picture-History Book,* Opryland USA, 1984.

Tosches, Nick, *Country: The Biggest Music in America,* Stein and Day, 1977.

Vecsey, George, *Coal Miner's Daughter,* Warner Books, 1976.

Wolfe, Charles K., *Kentucky Country: Folk and Country Music of Kentucky,* University Press of Kentucky, 1982.

——, *Tennessee Strings: The Story of Country Music in Tennessee,* University of Tennessee Press, 1977.

Articles

Billboard, selected issues.

Closeup, (newsletter of the Country Music Association), selected issues.

Country News, selected issues.

Country Rhythms, selected issues.

JEMF Quarterly, selected issues.

Journal of American Folklore, selected issues.

Journal of Country Music (published by the Country Music Foundation), selected issues.

Reports and Studies

Editorial Research Reports, "Rock Music Business," 1977 Vol. I, p. 433.

Graphics: Cover, inside illustrations by Assistant Art Director Robert O. Redding; pp. 25, 33 photos, courtesy of Opryland USA; p. 31 photos courtesy of the Country Music Foundation Library and Media Center, Nashville, Tenn.; p. 37, Emmylou Harris by Jim McGuire, Ricky Scaggs by Leonard Kamsler and Earl Scruggs by Norman Seeff.

TOURISM'S ECONOMIC IMPACT

by

Marc Leepson

May 4 1984

Editor's Note: Congress in 1984 did not complete action on legislation that would have set up a pilot program to encourage tourism by allowing tourists from some foreign countries to enter the United States without visas *(see p. 49)*. The provision was attached to omnibus immigration legislation, which died when House and Senate conferees were unable to agree on a compromise. Supporters of the visa relaxation have said they would try again to get Congress to approve the pilot program.

TOURISM'S ECONOMIC IMPACT

NATIONAL TOURISM WEEK begins May 27, and this year the travel industry is cautiously optimistic that it will have something to celebrate. During the 1981-82 recession, travel and tourism businesses fared better than many parts of the economy, but certain segments of the industry — notably hotels, motels, amusement parks and airlines — were hard hit. The industry as a whole rebounded in 1983, and is predicting that 1984 will be a good year for tourism in the United States.

Two special events should give a boost to the industry this year. More than 11 million people are expected to attend the 1984 Louisiana World Exposition, pumping an estimated $2.4 billion into New Orleans' economy during the fair's five-month run, which begins May 12. Seven million people are expected at the July 28-Aug. 12 Summer Olympic Games in Los Angeles; they should spend between $2 billion and $4 billion.

"We anticipate that travel is going to go up in both 1984 and 1985," said Donna Tuttle, who heads the U.S. Travel and Tourism Administration in the Commerce Department.[1] Tuttle predicts a 3 percent industry growth rate, which she attributes to the economic recovery, the World's Fair and the Olympics. Douglas C. Frechtling, director of the privately operated U.S. Travel Data Center, expects "we will see a considerable rise in vacation travel in 1984. As jobs and incomes continue to increase at high rates and prices remain relatively stable, Americans will once again turn to their favorite use of vacation time, travel away from home."[2]

American travel and tourism businesses earned about $200 billion in 1983, making travel and tourism the second largest retail industry in the country.[3] Nearly seven million Americans work directly or indirectly in travel and tourism, and the industry is of prime economic importance in most large cities and in all but a handful of states (see box, p. 45). "Tourism is definitely a major, major industry," said James Gaffigan, executive director of the Travel and Tourism Government Affairs

---

[1] Remarks by Tuttle and others quoted in this report, unless otherwise indicated, come from interviews with the author.

[2] Speaking at the 1984 Travel Outlook Forum, sponsored by the U.S. Travel Data Center, the Travel and Tourism Research Association and the Travel Industry Association of America, Dec. 12, 1983, in Arlington, Va.

[3] Preliminary data from the U.S. Travel Data Center.

Council. "We're the second largest employer in the United States behind health services. We're also the second largest retail business behind food sales, and in front of automotive sales. And we're the third largest earner of foreign currency behind grains and chemicals." [4]

Drop in American Share of World Tourism

Despite this upbeat economic assessment, travel industry executives are particularly concerned about one aspect of their business: the declining U.S. share of the $110 billion international tourism market. After 20 years of annual increases, the number of foreign tourists visiting the United States declined in 1982 and again last year when 21.6 million foreign travelers came to this country. At the same time, the number of Americans traveling overseas in 1983 increased by 7 percent over 1982, to 24.5 million. The United States drew 13.6 percent of the world's international tourists in 1976; in 1983 the U.S. share of the world tourism market fell to 10.1 percent *(see table, p. 47)*. Industry analysts say that each percent of the world tourism market equals about $1 billion in receipts, $165 million in federal, state and local tax revenues and 28,500 jobs. "We project that if America would return to its 13 percent share, we could provide $273 million more in federal tax revenues over three years and create some 55,000 jobs," William H. Edwards, president of the hotels division of Hilton Hotels Corp. and chairman of the Travel Industry Association of America, said at a December 1983 travel industry conference.

Travel analysts believe that economic conditions were the primary reason for American losses in the international tourism arena. Recovery from the worldwide economic recession was slower than expected, which held tourism down. Government statistics show that in 1983 the entire world tourism market grew by only 0.5 percent over 1982 and international tourist spending increased by only 2.1 percent. Moreover, the continued strength of the U.S. dollar against most foreign currencies cuts two ways to hurt the American market. The strong dollar means that foreign travel for Americans (especially to Europe and Mexico) is relatively inexpensive and that travel in the United States for foreigners is more expensive than ever.

Many in the U.S. travel industry believe a third factor that hurts this country is the federal government's failure to aggressively advertise the United States as a vacation spot for foreign tourists. Overseas tourism promotion, Gaffigan said, "is the only way that governments compete against governments. The pri-

---

[4] The Travel and Tourism Government Affairs Council is a Washington, D.C., trade organization made up of 28 national tourism organizations and associations. It is affiliated with the Travel Industry Association of America.

The Fragmented Travel Industry

Unlike other big American industries such as steel, coal or automobile manufacturing, which deal with one basic product, the American travel industry is very fragmented. It includes not only multibillion-dollar airlines and hotel chains, but also travel agencies, "mom and pop" motels, car rental agencies, commercial campgrounds, restaurants, bars, tour bus operators, amusement parks, convention centers and others. About one million individual businesses make up the industry.

"An overlooked thing about the industry is that it is really small business," said Vivian Deuschl of the federal U.S. Travel and Tourism Administration (USTTA). "People might think of the Hiltons or the Marriotts, and they're a very important part of it. But basically more than 95 percent of the businesses in travel and tourism are small businesses."

Analysts say that the industry's highly diverse nature has caused policymakers and the general public to underestimate the economic impact of travel and tourism. "People don't tend to look at tourism as an economic activity," said Randy Wagner, director of the Wyoming Travel Commission. "It's considered a recreational activity. They forget the economic value that it provides to the states and the nation." James Gaffigan, executive director of the Travel and Tourism Government Affairs Council, said, "People always look at the segments, and when they finally realize the pie, it's a damn big industry."

vate sector [spends] conservatively about $150 million promoting its own products, whether it's Holiday Inn, Hilton, Pan Am, TWA, et cetera. Nobody is promoting America as a generic product. . . . International tourism has a potential. It's just a question of how we can work with the federal government in promoting this in the self interest of the national economy."

Federal Promotional, Marketing Efforts

The first federally funded foreign tourism agency was the U.S. Travel Service (USTS), which was created within the Department of Commerce in 1961.[5] The agency's first project was revival of a modest "Visit U.S.A." program set up in 1960 by President Dwight D. Eisenhower. USTS distributed American travel literature overseas and made mailing lists of travel agents in foreign countries available to the American travel industry. But it did little else to advertise the United States abroad. After years of complaints from the travel industry about the agency's ineffectiveness, Congress passed the National Tourism Policy Act in 1981. That law replaced USTS with an upgraded agency, the U.S. Travel and Tourism Administration (USTTA). The new agency is headed by an under secretary of

---

[5] See "Tourist Dollar Gap," *E.R.R.*, 1966 Vol. I, pp. 359-378.

commerce for travel and tourism appointed by the president and confirmed by the Senate.[6]

The USTTA was directed to expand overseas promotional and marketing efforts. But the travel industry maintains that the agency has not gotten enough support from the Reagan administration. In 1983, for example, Reagan requested $5.4 million for USTTA operations in fiscal 1984. Congress, which was convinced that the agency needed more funds to do its job effectively, appropriated more than twice that amount — $12 million. For fiscal 1985, the administration has requested an $8.6 million budget for USTTA. "Money has always been a question in the history of this agency," said Tuttle, who was sworn in as under secretary Dec. 13, 1983. "This is a time of great deficits when everyone is looking at government spending and we want to keep government lean and trim."

Tuttle had no direct experience in the travel and tourism business when she took over as USTTA head five months ago. She had been a political campaign manager and fund-raiser in California and also had run her own small business, an interior design firm. Despite her lack of direct experience, Tuttle's leadership of USTTA has received wide praise from travel industry officials and members of Congress. "My personal perception and the perception that I hear voiced most frequently these days is that Secretary Tuttle in the short time she has been in office is doing a remarkable job," said Eric Peterson of the U.S. Senate Tourism Caucus. "She has brought a sense of organization, leadership and dedication to that post.... She has gone out of her way to win over the support of the industry and has gone to extraordinary lengths to curry the support and interest of members of Congress." James Gaffigan of the Travel and Tourism Government Affairs Council characterized Tuttle as "a very dynamic woman." Tuttle "has gone out, talked to the entire industry, has a lot of ideas and is running a good shop over there," he said.

Under Tuttle's leadership the USTTA is emphasizing market research and promotional programs. USTTA's Office of Research, for example, recently published the results of a survey of international air passengers who traveled during the first six months of 1983. The survey indicated that California was the most popular destination for foreign visitors, followed by New York, Florida and Hawaii. More than half of the foreign tourists visited only one U.S. state; about a quarter of the visitors spent time in three or more states. The survey also found that the average annual family income of visitors to the United States

---

[6] See *1981 CQ Almanac*, pp. 574-575.

Declining U.S. Share of World Tourism

Year	Foreign Spending in United States	U.S. Share of World Tourism Market	U.S. Spending on Overseas Promotion
1976	$ 5.7 billion	13.0%	$ 7.8 million
1977	6.2 billion	11.6	8.7 million
1978	7.2 billion	11.0	9.2 million
1979	8.3 billion	10.6	10.0 million
1980	10.1 billion	11.0	5.8 million
1981	12.2 billion	11.5	5.8 million
1982	11.7 billion	10.6	5.5 million
1983	11.7 billion*	10.1	5.5 million

*Estimated

Sources: World Tourism Organization, U.S. Department of Commerce

was about $44,000, compared with $57,000 for Americans traveling overseas during that time, and that the average foreign visitor spent about $1,100 in the United States. Nearly 40 percent of the tourists came from Europe and 29 percent from the Far East, including 1.45 million from Japan. Twenty percent were first-time visitors. "From that information we can determine where all these international visitors are coming from and what their destinations are and how much money they spend," Tuttle said. "That determines a lot about where we are going to go, what countries we're going to concentrate [our promotional efforts] on."

Cooperation of Public and Private Sectors

USTTA also helps individual state tourism bureaus attract foreign tourists. The agency sends state tourism brochures to its offices in Canada, England, France, Germany, Japan and Mexico, where the promotional literature is translated and distributed to foreign travel agents at no cost to the states. USTTA also has drafted a model state tourism policy law to emphasize the economic importance of tourism. USTTA conducts familiarization tours in the United States for foreign tour operators, travel agents and travel writers. "Last year $111 million of literally free advertising was written about America by travel journalists," said Vivian Deuschl of the USTTA.

The agency is redesigning its own brochures on traveling in the United States and is redoing a film to be aired on foreign television stations and used in USTTA promotional seminars. The agency will unveil a new promotional theme by the end of

1984. The new slogan, Donna Tuttle said, "is going to be something very simple [because] it's got to be translated into different languages. 'See America.' 'Travel America.' 'Visit America.' These are some of the ones being used now in the overseas markets by the individual directors." The theme, Tuttle said, will help American cities, states and the private travel industry "tie into a strong, coordinated promotional effort through USTTA in overseas markets. Industry is already out there spending money. We'd like states to get out there some more. By coordinating the effort and all of us hitting the same kind of generic theme of selling America, I think that can make more impact than anything."

Another of USTTA's goals is to work more closely with the private travel and tourism industry. "We've looked at other countries — Canada, Ireland, Australia, Spain — and they're good [at promoting international tourism] because they have a very close, coordinated program between private and public sectors," Tuttle said. "That's what our goal is, too. We think it works and a coordinated push really makes a difference."

Industry groups and businesses have worked with USTTA in recent years, providing or transporting free of charge brochures, maps, folders and pamphlets.[7] A group of marketing experts from the private sector is drawing up a plan to help USTTA increase international tourism.[8] "What we're trying to do is give USTTA a better understanding of what's out there, who our competitors are, what are promising markets, what countries have potential that we haven't explored," said Gaffigan of the Travel and Tourism Government Affairs Council. "Then we'll sit down with policymakers, and make them aware of the fact that there is a potential. This has not been done in the past."

Both the USTTA and the travel industry are working to change the requirement that tourists from all foreign countries (except Canada and Mexico) obtain visas before entering the United States. Most Western nations require only passports for visiting tourists. Even in communist Yugoslavia, American tourists can get visas at border crossings merely by showing their passports to immigration officials. On the other hand, foreigners planning to visit the United States must obtain visas before leaving home. Long delays and bureaucratic snafus as understaffed State Department offices overseas try to keep up with visa paperwork have discouraged many foreigners — particularly Europeans — from visiting the United States.

---

[7] These include the National Tour Association, the American Bus Association, the American Hotel and Motel Association, American Express Co., Pan American World Airways, Trans World Airlines and the American Telephone & Telegraph Co.

[8] The group, known as the International Marketing Plan Development Committee, will complete its work on a five-year plan sometime this year.

Legislation that would set up a pilot program allowing visitors from eight countries whose rates of visa fraud are below 2 percent to enter the United States without visas is pending in Congress. The program "would help a number of countries abroad that provide us with a good number of overseas visitors and make it easier for those people to come to the United States without as much red tape," Gaffigan said. Although the visa-waiver provisions are themselves not particularly controversial, they have been attached to the larger and hotly contested Immigration Reform and Control bill. Capitol Hill observers say that Congress may not pass the measure in this election year.

Foreign Competition

THE FEDERAL EFFORT to attract international tourists pales in comparison with programs in other countries. Among the governments that outspent the United States in tourism promotion last year are both developing nations (among them Colombia, Jamaica, Tunisia, Costa Rica, Malaysia and Bermuda) and developed countries (such as Greece, Spain, Belgium, Holland, Italy, West Germany and Canada). In 1983, the federal government ranked 30th in the amount spent on tourism *(see box, p. 51).*

Measured on a per capita basis the average developed country spent over 70 times as much as the U.S. government on tourism promotion in 1983.[9] Not only are other countries spending more than the United States, said William Edwards, national chairman of the Travel Industry Association of America, but "their efforts are increasing, while ours are going down."[10] Gaffigan agreed: "If you look in *Time* magazine or *Newsweek* you see very, very sophisticated ads from Canada and you'll see them from England, Germany, et cetera. In addition to that, there is an enormous amount of competition from Third World nations."

There is evidence that the heavy advertising is paying off. Nations that promote tourism aggressively have found that increased tourism promotion budgets translate into higher tourism receipts within a few years. The Madrid-based World Tour-

[9] Statistics from "Tourism Fact Sheets: A Resource Kit," a compilation of travel statistics from the World Tourism Council and other sources, published by the Travel and Tourism Government Affairs Council.

[10] Speaking Dec. 12, 1983, at the Travel Outlook Forum in Arlington, Va.

ism Organization reported the following results from six nations
that stepped up travel promotion budgets in 1976:

Country	Increase in Advertising Budget, 1976-81	Increase in Tourism Receipts, 1976-81
Canada	$3.8 million (23%)	$643 million (38%)
France	$4.7 million (156%)	$5.1 billion (164%)
Singapore	$1.3 million (28%)	$602 million (213%)
Spain	$9.9 million (83%)	$3.9 billion (126%)
Sri Lanka	$992 thousand (177%)	$69 million (245%)
West Germany	$7.0 million (24%)	$3.4 billion (106%)

A record number of Americans — 24.5 million — traveled to
foreign countries last year — a 7 percent increase over 1982.
Industry analysts say several factors contributed to the great
vacation exodus: aggressive promotion by foreign tourist bureaus, generally lower trans-Atlantic air fares, the unprecedented strength of the U.S. dollar against the Mexican peso and
most European currencies, and what the travel industry calls
"pent-up" consumer demand in the wake of postponed travel
plans during two years of recession. According to USTTA statistics, 2.3 million Americans visited Great Britain in 1983, a 30
percent increase over 1982; more than four million went to
Mexico, a 22 percent increase; and 11.3 million went to Canada,
a 3 percent increase. Australia, China, India, Israel, Jamaica,
Japan, the Philippines and New Zealand also welcomed thousands of American tourists in 1983.

Effect of Strong U.S. Dollar on 'Travel Gap'

European advertising in the United States last year stressed
how inexpensively Americans could travel on the continent.
"Europe! The Grandest Holiday of All. Now More Affordable
Than Ever." So read an advertisement distributed widely in the
United States by the European Travel Commission — an inter-
European group that promotes travel on the continent rather
than in any specific country. An Iberian Airlines ad that appeared in American newspapers and magazines read: "Say Hello
to a Real Good Buy: Iberia's Spain.... With today's exchange
rate, the time is perfect for you and your dollars to enjoy all
Spain has to offer."

American travelers spent a record $19.2 billion in foreign
countries in 1983, a 12 percent increase over the previous year.
Receipts from foreign tourists in this country, on the other
hand, came to $13.8 billion last year. The $5.4 billion deficit in
what the Commerce Department calls the "international travel
dollar account" — also known as the "travel gap" and the
"tourist dollar gap" — was 60 percent higher than the 1982

National Spending on Tourism

(In millions)

The following chart shows the amounts spent by national government tourist organizations similar to the United States Travel and Tourism Administration.

Country	1983 Spending	Country	1983 Spending
1. Mexico	$ 182.1	16. Colombia	$ 13.8
2. Czechoslovakia	134.8	17. West Germany	13.5
3. Brazil	78.6	18. Hungary	12.8
4. Greece	69.1	19. Bermuda	12.3
5. Spain	61.1*	20. Israel	12.3
6. South Korea	59.0	21. Netherlands	12.3
7. Switzerland	47.4*	22. Trinidad & Tobago	11.3
8. Canada	39.3	23. United Kingdom	11.2*
9. Italy	36.5	24. Australia	10.6
10. Jamaica	29.5	25. Finland	9.3
11. Belgium	25.6	26. Japan	9.2
12. France	25.2	27. Costa Rica	8.7
13. India	24.3	28. Malaysia	8.4
14. Tunisia	19.9	29. Philippines	8.4
15. Egypt	15.7	30. United States	7.6

*Estimated
Sources: World Tourism Organization and Travel and Tourism Government Affairs Council

deficit of $3.4 billion.[11] Government travel analysts predict that the improving worldwide economic climate, the World's Fair and the Summer Olympic Games will lead to a modest rise in international arrivals in this country in 1984. But if the dollar remains strong, Americans probably will continue to travel abroad in large numbers and there likely will be another multi-billion-dollar deficit in the U.S. travel dollar account.

"If the dollar weakens in 1984 . . . , the visit-USA market from overseas could grow 5 percent," Frechtling of the U.S. Travel Data Center said. "I expect, instead, the dollar will not weaken significantly against European or Western Hemisphere currencies. However, foreign arrivals from abroad will grow 2 to 3 percent as European economic recovery finally gathers steam and Asian economies continue to pace the world. South American nations, struggling with enormous debt burdens, will remain depressed areas for travel to the U.S. for at least another year or

[11] The $13.8 billion was made up of $11.2 billion spent by visitors while in the United States and $2.6 billion paid to U.S. airlines for transportation.

two." [12] Don Wynegar, director of USTTA's Office of Research, predicted in December that the "growth rate" of American tourists heading overseas will "moderate somewhat" in 1984.

In the past when the international travel account was in arrears, government officials urged Americans to take more vacations in this country. In 1966, for example, when the travel gap was expected to reach $2 billion, Treasury Secretary Henry H. Fowler suggested that Americans would be following the path of "responsible restraint" by postponing "wherever possible travel abroad and substituting travel in this country." There was even talk that year of imposing a special tax of $10 for each day an American spent outside the country. No such tax was levied, however, and government and travel industry officials today do not discourage Americans from taking overseas vacations. "The travel industry basically believes you're going to travel and you'll travel out [of the country] and you'll travel in," Gaffigan said. "That's part of a free democracy."

Successes of Canadian, Irish Ad Campaigns

Travel analysts say that Canada and Ireland have two of the world's most effective tourism marketing and promotion programs. The national tourism effort in Canada is the direct responsibility of a Cabinet-level department, the Ministry of State for Small Business and Tourism, currently headed by David P. Smith. For the 1983-84 fiscal year, which ended April 1, the national tourism office, Tourism Canada, had a marketing budget of nearly $35 million and an advertising budget of some $27 million.[13] About $18 million of the advertising budget was aimed at the United States, where the agency maintains 14 offices. Statistics show that tourism accounted for some $16.5 billion in revenues in 1983, nearly 5 percent of Canada's GNP. Tourism is the fifth largest earner of foreign currency for the country, and is responsible for one-tenth of all Canadian jobs. About 100,000 businesses are directly involved in tourism. "It is vitally important to our economy," said Georgia Maclean, a Tourism Canada counselor at the Canadian Embassy in Washington.

Canada's primary tourism market is, of course, the United States. More Americans go to Canada than to any other foreign country; 11 million stayed at least one night there last year and spent $2.7 billion. Conversely the United States is the favorite vacation spot for Canadians. Nearly 12 million visited this country for longer than a day in 1983, and the nation had a tourist

---

[12] Writing in the U.S. Travel Data Center's publication, *Director's Letter*, February 1984, p. 5.
[13] All figures used in this section are in Canadian dollars. One American dollar currently equals about $1.28 in Canadian currency.

San Francisco's California Street cable car — an enduring tourist attraction

dollar gap with the United States of about $2 billion. That deficit was one reason behind a recently announced stepped-up promotional effort to entice more Americans to take vacations north of the border. "No other foreign country is as popular a vacation destination for Americans as Canada," Minister Smith said in *Travel Times*, an advertising supplement widely distributed in American newspapers in March. "And there's never been a better year than this year! So come on up."

Tourism Canada's American advertising campaigns are based on extensive marketing research and are aimed at specific segments of the American population. Advertisements in skiing magazines, for example, promote Canada's ski resorts; ads in outdoors magazines extol the nation's hunting and fishing areas. Some advertising is intended to change Americans' image of Canada. A recent ad campaign, for example, was designed "to

let people know that we're not under snow all year round," said
Carol Bruce, manager of market planning for Tourism Canada's
marketing branch in Ottawa. Marketing research "discovered
that people had an impression that Canada consists mainly of
wilderness," Bruce said. "So we wanted to let people know that
we have urban products to offer as well."

Unlike USTTA, which seeks only to attract foreign travelers
to the United States, Tourism Canada runs several programs
within Canada itself. "Some are advertising programs designed
to encourage Canadians to visit other parts of their own country," Carol Bruce said. Others try to heighten awareness of the
importance of tourism to the nation's economy. The effort to
encourage Canadians to vacation at home has been only partially successful. "Canadians have historically been, and I believe always will be, great travelers," said Maclean. "We travel a
great deal outside our own borders. I think nothing short of
barbed wire across the border will keep us home. . . ."

Ireland has had little trouble convincing its citizens of the
economic importance of tourism. "Tourism is probably more
important to the economy of Ireland than it is to any European
country," said Cairbre Hally, regional sales executive for the
Irish Tourist Board in Washington, D.C. "It ranks third in
importance to agriculture and industry — a very close third."
The Irish Tourist Board (known in Ireland as *Bord Fáilte*), is a
semi-autonomous agency funded by the federal government. Its
mission is not only to attract foreign travelers to Ireland, but
also to develop the industry within the country. "This goes as
far as having cash grants for the development of accommoda-
tions and tourist facilities — things like cruising on the Shan-
non — to developing angling centers," Hally said. "It also
includes things like producing the guidebooks to accommoda-
tions, eating, angling, you name it." The Irish Tourist Board has
statutory authority over many parts of the Irish tourist industry. Hotels, for example, cannot operate in the country until
they are registered with the tourist board, which inspects and
grades each hotel on quality.

Of the more than two million tourists who visited Ireland last
year, nearly half came from Great Britain. But the second-
largest group — 277,000 visitors from the United States —
spent the most money in Ireland. Accordingly, the Irish Tourist
Board operates an extensive marketing and promotion effort in
this country, maintaining offices in New York City, Boston,
Washington, D.C., Los Angeles, San Francisco and Chicago. The
board brings Irish tourist industry officials to this country to
meet with U.S. travel agents, sponsors trips by American
journalists to Ireland and runs consumer advertising campaigns.

The current campaign, which began in February, is "aimed at overcoming a lack of awareness of the variety of Irish vacation appeals," an Irish Tourist Board report said.[14] Using the slogan "Ireland: The Unexpected Pleasures," the campaign consists of newspaper and magazine ads showing well-known and not-so-well-known aspects of Ireland. In one ad, an aerial view of the lush green rolling countryside is pictured next to a chef surrounded by a lavish variety of food. The idea is to dispel the notion that good food cannot be found in Ireland.

These efforts have brought Ireland an international reputation for aggressiveness and success in tourism promotion and development. Hally explained some of the reasons for that success. "We're a small country. A lot of people have the wrong impressions about our country," he said. "We can't bring everyone to our country to show them initially what it's like, so we do certainly have to fight a lot harder than other countries to sell tourism. And we're not into the three 'S's' tourism as [are] many countries: the sun, sand and sex.... We can sell loads of sand; we've plenty of beaches. We can't guarantee the sun; the other aspect we don't mention."

Tourism in America

TRAVEL AND TOURISM are extremely important economic factors in many states. In 39 of them, the travel and tourism industry ranks either first, second or third in terms of revenue. Only eight of the 50 states received less than $1 billion in travel-generated business in 1981, the last year for which complete statistics are available. California, the leader by far with $26.7 billion in travel revenues, was one of 10 states collecting more than $5.5 billion. Eleven states received between $3 billion and $5 billion *(see table, pp. 56-57)*.

Nevada is the state most dependent on tourism. About 30 percent of the state's workers are employed by the travel industry, most of which is centered on gambling. In Las Vegas a strike by 17,000 hotel and casino workers that began April 2 could have grave implications for the economy of the entire state. According to *Business Week*, business at the largest hotels has fallen by 70 percent. Some hotels have cut their rates to lure visitors and hired non-union labor to keep their doors open,

---

[14] "The United States Market: Tourism to Ireland 1984," Irish Tourist Board, February 1984.

The Booming Travel Business . . .

State	No. of Jobs	Rank*	% of All Jobs	Domestic Travelers	Foreign Travelers	Total Tax Receipts
	Employees			**Revenues** (in millions)		
Ala.	34,000	(7)	2.5%	$ 1,230	$ 20	$ 112.3
Alaska	13,000	(1)	7.1	784	4	138.2
Ariz.	66,000	(1)	6.3	2,672	742	252.2
Ark.	44,000	(2)	6.0	1,535	—	118.5
Calif.	515,000	(2)	5.2	23,942	2,824	2,720.7
Colo.	99,000	(1)	7.6	3,684	202	439.2
Conn.	38,000	(10)	2.6	2,096	127	296.7
Del.	17,000	(2)	6.6	462	39	51.6
Fla.	332,000	(1)	8.9	13,812	2,062	1,290.2
Ga.	98,000	(3)	4.4	4,474	192	428.5
Hawaii	57,000	(1)	14.1	2,247	509	240.8
Idaho	29,000	(1)	8.8	826	30	78.5
Ill.	127,000	(8)	2.7	5,524	489	673.7
Ind.	66,000	(7)	3.1	2,391	49	267.0
Iowa	51,000	(3)	4.6	1,610	5	141.0
Kan.	41,000	(3)	4.4	1,506	92	137.7
Ky.	45,000	(3)	3.8	2,042	65	183.3
La.	71,000	(3)	4.3	3,144	211	305.5
Maine	38,000	(1)	9.0	1,199	136	106.4
Md.	71,000	(3)	4.0	2,736	104	355.3
Mass.	94,000	(6)	3.5	4,264	328	521.2
Mich.	124,000	(5)	3.7	5,259	258	601.3
Minn.	110,000	(2)	6.3	3,964	149	489.5
Miss.	29,000	(4)	3.6	1,047	4	100.2
Mo.	103,000	(2)	5.3	4,078	167	441.2

*Rank among all employers in state.

but, as one union official said, "there is no question the impact has been substantial."

Hawaii, which also is heavily dependent on the tourist trade, is looking for ways to revitalize the industry as well as to diversify its economy. Last year, according to the Hawaii Visitors Bureau, more than four million people visited the islands and spent nearly $4 billion. Although both figures represent increases from 1982, the rate of growth has slipped in recent years and analysts predict that tourism growth rates will continue to be below the national average for the next few years. This decline in tourism is attributed largely to the affordability of air travel. Once based on the wealthy tourist who arrived by ship and stayed for several weeks, Hawaii's tourist trade now serves fewer wealthy travelers who stay for shorter periods and spend less.

... Tourism by State, 1981

State	Employees			Revenues (in millions)		
	No. of Jobs	Rank*	% of All Jobs	Domestic Travelers	Foreign Travelers	Total Tax Receipts
Mont.	21,000	(1)	7.5%	$ 626	$ 68	$ 45.0
Neb.	33,000	(2)	5.4	1,063	—	109.7
Nev.	123,000	(1)	29.9	5,454	735	645.6
N.H.	31,000	(1)	7.8	1,011	47	67.3
N.J.	160,000	(2)	5.2	6,416	193	736.6
N.M.	37,000	(1)	7.7	1,221	21	108.5
N.Y.	262,000	(3)	3.6	12,456	2,099	1,847.8
N.C.	101,000	(2)	4.2	3,803	64	322.9
N.D.	18,000	(2)	7.2	647	8	56.2
Ohio	133,000	(8)	3.1	5,596	233	581.2
Okla.	63,000	(2)	5.2	2,338	100	230.6
Ore.	55,000	(3)	5.4	2,045	108	177.4
Pa.	180,000	(3)	3.8	6,923	385	776.3
R.I.	11,000	(8)	2.6	366	15	45.3
S.C.	68,000	(2)	5.7	2,342	183	214.2
S.D.	15,000	(2)	6.2	456	71	44.4
Tenn.	73,000	(2)	4.2	2,652	114	241.0
Texas	273,000	(4)	4.4	12,604	1,502	1,152.0
Utah	39,000	(1)	6.9	1,198	66	123.9
Vt.	36,000	(1)	17.4	964	97	84.7
Va.	83,000	(3)	3.9	3,326	243	307.4
Wash.	59,000	(4)	3.7	2,541	425	258.9
W.Va.	31,000	(3)	4.9	1,092	12	88.5
Wis.	108,000	(3)	5.6	3,373	192	346.8
Wyo.	20,000	(2)	8.9	736	33	62.6

Source: U.S. Travel Data Center, Travel and Tourism Government Affairs Council

State Approaches to Encouraging Travel

Hawaii is trying to rekindle its tourism business through large-scale international promotion. The state was second only to Florida in money spent on advertising in foreign markets in 1982-83, according to data compiled by the Travel and Tourism Government Affairs Council. Hawaii spent $400,000 trying to lure foreign visitors to the islands in 1982-83. Nearly a third of that total was aimed at Japan, where the state maintains a tourism office in Tokyo. Hawaii also promotes itself heavily in the continental United States. The state runs regional tourism offices in five U.S. cities: New York, Chicago, San Francisco, Los Angeles and Washington, D.C.

Other states have mounted successful advertising campaigns. Washington, for example, began a $4.5 million national promotion campaign in 1982 with the theme of "See America's Other Washington." The next year more than 14 million people visited the state, a 6.9 percent increase over 1982. The state realized $277.2 million in tax revenues in 1983, a 4 percent increase in tourism-related jobs and a 10 percent jump in hotel and motel receipts. A heavy promotional effort aimed at Asian countries, combined with newly inaugurated air service between Seattle and Hong Kong and Tokyo, boosted international tourist arrivals 17.5 percent in 1983.

The 50 states collectively spend far more than the federal government does each year on tourism promotion. According to the U.S. Travel Data Center, the states spent $147 million on tourism promotion in the 1983-84 fiscal year, a 15 percent increase over 1982. The average state spent $982,900 on tourism promotion. Florida had the largest budget, $8.9 million. Some states band together in marketing cooperatives to promote themselves overseas. One such group, known as Foremost West, promotes Arizona, Colorado, New Mexico, Utah and Wyoming. "We take part in most of the international trade shows," Wyoming Travel Commission Director Randy Wagner said of the group. "We do periodic trade missions to various countries. We print a lot of literature in foreign languages and distribute it both through Foremost West and through the USTTA outlets [overseas].... We also host a number of familiarization tours where we bring foreign tour operators, travel agents and journalists over to this country and travel them through our states to show them the attractions we have." Other regional marketing groups are made up of states in the Great Lakes region, the South and New England.

New Popularity of City Convention Centers

Many American cities also depend heavily on tourism. New York, Los Angeles, Washington, D.C., Las Vegas, New Orleans and San Francisco attract millions of visitors each year and reap billions of dollars annually in tourism revenue. Tourism also is an important economic factor in cities that do not have attractions to compare with Broadway, Hollywood, the French Quarter or gambling casinos. What cities such as Baton Rouge, Cincinnati, Cleveland, Detroit, Pittsburgh and San Antonio do have to attract large numbers of American visitors are convention centers. New York, Los Angeles and the other top tourist attractions, of course, also have convention centers; there are more than 100 across the country.

Convention centers host thousands of trade shows, association and union meetings, conventions and special events such as concerts and ballet performances every year. These, in turn, draw thousands of out-of-town visitors who pump money into local tourism-oriented businesses — hotels, restaurants, night clubs, taxicabs and other forms of transportation. Among the newest is the recently completed $95 million, 15-acre Convention Center in New Orleans. The huge center — which features a 100- by 300-foot lagoon in its Great Hall — will host dozens of special events during this summer's World's Fair. The Convention Center already has scheduled trade shows and meetings after Nov. 11 when the fair closes. Convention centers can mean "big business for urban centers or any geographic area," said Frank Carrell, vice president of the Convention and Visitors Bureau of Greater Cleveland. Visitors to that city and surrounding Cuyahoga County spent more than $1 billion in 1982, according to a study done by the U.S. Travel Data Center. The study found that travel and tourism accounted for some 23,000 jobs in the county, including about 9,000 in the city of Cleveland. The county received $16.7 million in local tax revenues that year; the city, $5.8 million. "It's interesting to note that a city like Cleveland and the county that it is in are not noted as great visitor destinations nor visitor centers," Carrell said. "But the city and the county ranked the highest in the state of Ohio [in tourism revenues] in the study done by the U.S. Travel Data Center."

In 1984 Cleveland will host some 200 conventions, including a Society of Manufacturing Engineers trade show that is expected to attract some 25,000 participants, a National Urban League meeting with some 10,000 delegates, a United Steel Workers convention with as many as 8,000 delegates and a meeting of the American Federation of Government Employees with 5,000 delegates. Carrell's organization estimates that delegates to these and other conventions and trade shows each will spend about $370 during an average 3.9-day stay in Cleveland this year. A show with 10,000 delegates would therefore put $3.7 million in revenue into the city's tourism industry.

Convention centers also benefit cities in less tangible ways. The events that take place in convention centers "affect your quality of life to a certain degree," said Norman Bermes, president of the International Association of Convention and Visitor Bureaus. "You can attract better entertainment — the more seats you have, the less cost per seat it will be for some of the larger entertainers. . . . These are things that make it enjoyable to live in a community, make a good quality of life."

Tourism officials in cities across the country agree that 1984 will be a profitable year. The industry, Bermes said, should fare well this year primarily because Americans have strong feelings about vacations. The "mindset of the American," he said, is " 'I've earned it. I deserve it. I'm going to take it.' " During economic hard times, Americans still take vacations, but they stay closer to home. During this year of general economic recovery, Americans are likely to vacation longer and travel farther.

Selected Bibliography

Books

Gunn, Clare A., *Tourism Planning*, Crane-Russak, 1979.
Lundberg, Donald E., *The Tourist Business*, 4th ed., CBI, 1980.
MacCannell, Dean, *The Tourist*, Schocken Books, 1976.
Reilly, Robert T., *Travel and Tourism Marketing Techniques*, Merton House, 1980.

Articles

Demarest, Michael, *et al.*, "Americans Everywhere," *Time*, July 25, 1983.
DiLullo, Anthony J., "U.S. International Transactions, Third Quarter 1983," *Survey of Current Business*, December 1983.
Doan, Michael, "Great American Stampede to Vacation Overseas," *U.S. News & World Report*, July 18, 1983.
Gatty, Bob, "The Travel Industry Picks Up Speed," *Nation's Business*, August 1983.
Travel Log, newsletter of Travel and Tourism Government Affairs Council, selected issues.

Reports and Studies

Editorial Research Reports, "Tourism Boom," 1978 Vol. II, p. 521; "Leisure Business," 1973 Vol. I, p. 147; "Tourist Dollar Gap," 1966 Vol. I, p. 359.
Irish Tourist Board, "The United States Market: Tourism to Ireland, 1984," February 1984.
Travel and Tourism Government Affairs Council: "Tourism Fact Sheets: A Resource Kit," 1983; "State Fact Sheets: Economic Impact of Travel and Tourism in 1981," July 1983.
U.S. Department of Commerce, U.S. Travel and Tourism Administration: "Marketing Plan for Fiscal Year 1985," 1984; "International Travel to and from the United States: 1984 Outlook," Dec. 12, 1983; "Annual Report of the National Tourism Policy Council for Fiscal Year 1983," Dec. 27, 1983; "In-Flight Survey of International Air Travelers," March 1984.
U.S. Travel Data Center: "The 1982-83 Economic Review of Travel in America," 1983; "1984 Outlook for Travel and Tourism: Proceedings of the U.S. Travel Data Center's 1984 Travel Outlook Forum," 1984; *Director's Letter: Travel Analysis and Commentary*, selected issues.

Graphics: Cover illustration, internal graphics by Assistant Art Director Robert Redding.

NEW ERA
IN TV SPORTS

by

Marc Leepson

Sept. 7
1 9 8 4

NEW ERA IN
TV SPORTS

*Games enlist skill and intelligence, the utmost
concentration of purpose, on behalf of activities utterly useless, which make no contribution to the struggle of man against nature, to
the wealth or comfort of the community, or to
its physical survival.*

— Christopher Lasch

CHANCES ARE, most sports fans would agree with Lasch's
observation about the wider implications of sports in society. Yet games of sport are immensely popular throughout the
world — even if they have nothing to do with the physical
survival of the species. The United States is as sports-crazy as
any other nation. Witness the idolatrous treatment of the nation's athletes in the Summer Olympics; they were hailed as
heroes by everyone from the president to flag-waving citizens on
the street. Or the fervor with which people in Pennsylvania,
Texas and Ohio towns follow the fortunes of their high school
football teams. Or the fact that normal activity comes to a
virtual standstill in places such as Indiana and North Carolina
when the state university plays for the national collegiate
basketball championship. Or the wild public parades for Super
Bowl-winning football teams.

Every year tens of millions of Americans show up in person to
cheer the home teams. Yet their number is dwarfed by those
who stay home and follow sports on television. There is a wider
menu of sports events on TV today than ever before. Network
television, cable TV stations, regional pay cable networks and
local independent stations are giving over unprecedented
amounts of air time to sports. Take college football, for just one
example. A recent Supreme Court ruling "deregulated" the
televising of games, which had been controlled by the National
Collegiate Athletic Association *(see p. 69)*. As a result, the
number of college football games on TV this season will at least
double 1983's 89 telecasts.

Major-league baseball and college football were very popular
before the television era. But television thrust other sports,

especially professional football, basketball and hockey, into the national spotlight. The first televised sporting events — a University of Pennsylvania football game and a Columbia-Princeton baseball game — were broadcast on an experimental basis in 1938 and 1939. By the early 1950s games and the medium forged an alliance, and since then both have enjoyed unprecedented popularity. "Television," Christopher Lasch said, "did for these games what mass-journalism had done [in the 1920s] for baseball, elevating them to new heights of popularity and at the same time reducing them to entertainment."[1] At the same time, sports gave television an immeasurable boost. "Sports made television commercially successful," wrote educator-author Michael Novak. "No other motive is so frequently cited ... for shelling out money for a set...."[2]

The large and growing appetite for sports on the part of the American public has translated into big business for television — and for the sports teams, professional leagues and college conferences that sell broadcast rights. For example, during ABC's unprecedented 180-hour coverage of the Olympic Games July 28-Aug. 12, the average 30-second commercial in prime time sold for $260,000. Analysts say that ABC, which spent more than $325 million for broadcast rights and in production costs, still profited handsomely from the Olympics. Under the current $2 billion contract between the three major over-the-air networks (ABC, CBS and NBC) and the National Football League (NFL), commercials sell for $345,000 a minute. Broadcast rights — including radio, television and pay cable television — for major-league baseball have increased sixfold in the last decade to nearly $268 million in 1984, according to *Broadcasting* magazine *(see box, p. 75)*.

Television is in large measure responsible for the birth and limited success of the United States Football League (USFL), a professional rival to the NFL. In May 1982, months before the league had signed its first player, it sold network broadcast rights to ABC for two years for $18 million and cable rights to the Entertainment and Sports Programming Network (ESPN) for two years for $11 million. "Thus assured that the nation's premier sports network and a leading cable network would carry their pro football league, the [USFL owners] *then* set about assembling the league's remaining necessities — players, coaches, host cities, stadiums," wrote television analyst Ron Powers. "This was the cathode genesis of the United States Football League."[3] In June 1984 ESPN paid $71 million to the

[1] Christopher Lasch, *The Culture of Narcissism* (1978), p. 121.
[2] Michael Novak, *The Joy of Sports* (1976), p. 25.
[3] Ron Powers, *Supertube* (1984), p. 273.

ABC's Olympic Ratings

According to ABC, more than 180 million Americans, representing 90 percent of the nation's households, tuned in sometime during the 16 days of coverage of the Los Angeles Olympic Games, July 28-Aug. 12. This was the most U.S. viewers ever to watch any event on television. During that time ABC drew a larger audience than NBC and CBS combined, according to estimates by A. C. Nielsen Co. Nielsen ratings showed that an average of 45 percent of all television households tuned in to the Olympics during ABC's prime-time coverage. ABC announced that 97 million Americans watched the Aug. 12 closing ceremonies, the highest-rated event of the 16 days of Olympic coverage.

USFL for exclusive cable TV rights for three years beginning in 1985, according to industry observers. Under an option in its contract, ABC has offered the league some $15 million for non-cable broadcast rights for the 1985 season. The USFL is far from sound financially — observers say that only one team, the Tampa Bay Bandits, made a profit in 1984. But league attendance rose by an average of 9 percent last year. Television exposure is at least partially responsible for the attendance jump and TV revenues are almost totally responsible for the fact that the league is still in business.

Decline in Ratings; Fear of Overexposure

More sporting events than ever before are available on television. And more people than ever before are watching sports on television. Yet, ratings for some network and cable sporting events — including college basketball and college and professional football — have fallen in recent years. There are many reasons for the ratings decreases, but industry analysts say that a primary cause has been an "oversaturation" of sporting events on the airwaves. The over-the-air networks alone run about 1,500 hours of sports programming a year. Independent stations air thousands of local and regional professional and collegiate sporting events in towns and cities across the nation. And then there is the growing sports coverage provided on cable television. According to the National Cable Television Association, sports coverage is cable TV's "fastest growing program category."

At last count, 11 cable networks were broadcasting sporting events on a regular basis, including ESPN, the only 24-hour television network devoted primarily to sports. There also are 22 regional pay sports networks, most of which began operating in the last three years (see p. 77). The cable subscriber must pay an additional monthly fee to tune in to these regional

networks. They typically broadcast home games of local professional baseball, basketball and hockey teams. "There is
no question that there is an ever present danger of over-
exposure," said Alan Cole-Ford, an analyst with Paul Kagan
Associates, a cable TV consulting firm. More sports on
TV, Cole-Ford said, "has to begin to take a toll. Likely that
toll is going to be taken on the number of games [shown by]
local, commercial independents. Something's got to give somewhere to some degree. It is going to depend a lot on each
market." [4]

"We're mindful of the fact that, on the one hand, television
is probably the best marketing tool ever invented, so it's
important to be seen and be seen consistently," said Ed Desser,
director of broadcasting for the National Basketball Association (NBA). "Yet, the more people see on TV, the less inclined
they are going to be perhaps to go to as many games, or at least
to watch every game.... We think that moderation in the
amount of exposure is of some benefit." The league's new contract with WTBS, the Atlanta-based cable network, about
halves the number of NBA cable telecasts to be shown this
season. The contract gives WTBS exclusive cable rights to
NBA games. In the past, NBA games also had been shown on
cable on ESPN and the USA Network. WTBS, which had aired
virtually all of the Atlanta Hawks' 82 regular-season games in
the past, this year will show a mixed menu of about 75 NBA
contests. [5]

Even though cable broadcasts are being cut back, many other
NBA games will be available elsewhere on television. About 34
games (both regular season and playoff contests) will be shown
on CBS. The NBA also permits its 23 teams to negotiate their
own local broadcast arrangements with local independent stations and with regional pay cable networks. Next season 15
NBA teams[6] will be shown by the regional pay networks.

Cable Sport Strategies: USA and ESPN

At least one cable network is cutting back on the amount of
sports programming it carries. The USA Network went on the
air in September 1980 as an all-sports cable offshoot of the
Madison Square Garden Network, a regional pay cable service
in New York City. USA broadcast professional hockey and
basketball games from Madison Square Garden, added other

---

[4] Cole-Ford and others quoted in this report were interviewed by the author, unless
otherwise indicated.
[5] Ted Turner, the owner of WTBS, owns the Hawks and also the Atlanta Braves of major-
league baseball.
[6] The Boston Celtics, Chicago Bulls, Dallas Mavericks, Denver Nuggets, Detroit Pistons,
Houston Rockets, Los Angeles Lakers, Milwaukee Bucks, New Jersey Nets, New York
Knicks, Philadelphia 76ers, Phoenix Suns, San Antonio Spurs, Seattle Supersonics, Washington Bullets.

Sports On Cable

On a day chosen at random, Tuesday, Aug. 14, the following sporting events were broadcast nationwide on cable television:

Sport	Network	Program	Time*
Baseball	ESPN	Inside Baseball	11:30 p.m., 3:30 p.m.
	WGN	Cubs vs. Astros	8:35 p.m.
	WTBS	Pirates vs. Braves	7:35 p.m.
Boxing	ESPN	Welterweight title bout: Martin vs. Colome	12 noon; 7:30 p.m.
Football	ESPN	Canadian League: Montreal vs. Winnipeg	4 p.m.
	ESPN	Super Bowl X highlights	11:15 p.m.
Karate	ESPN	Jackson vs. Morrison	10 a.m.
Miscellaneous	ESPN	Sports Look	6:30 p.m.
	ESPN	Sports Woman	9:30 a.m.
Motor Sports	ESPN	Drag Racing	11:45 p.m.
	ESPN	Stock Car Racing	1:15 a.m.
	ESPN	Auto Racing	2:30 a.m.
	USA	Motorcycle Racing	12 midnight
Pool	ESPN	Crane vs. Caras	2:30 p.m.
	ESPN	Caras v. Moore	10 p.m.
Sports News	CNN	Sports Late Night	2:30 a.m.
	CNN	Sports Tonight	11:30 p.m.
	ESPN	Sports Center	4 times
Waterskiing	USA	Tournament of Champions	1 a.m.
Wrestling	USA	Tuesday Night Titans	8 p.m., 2 a.m.

*Eastern time for shows aired simultaneously in all time zones; for others local times.

Source: *USA Today*, Aug. 14, 1984.

sports events and beamed 24 hours of programming nationwide via cable. "On prime time just about every night of the week we ran some sort of a sports event," said Jim Zrake, USA's executive producer for sports. "We probably hit our peak, where we were doing something like 450-500 events a year around 1981. Ever since then we've tried to scale down." Only about 20 percent of the programming on USA, which is seen by some 24.3 million subscribers on about 4,000 cable systems nationwide, now consists of sports. Still, sports remain an important segment of USA's programming. "It's still a very high-profile item," Zrake said. "We're going to go after what we consider the top ticket items that we feel that people still want to watch."

ESPN, the cable network that shows the most sports by far, has no plans to cut back its sports coverage. ESPN, which began programming in September 1979, now has more than 30 million subscribers and is available on nearly 8,000 cable systems. "Our ratings are good. Our goal is a 2.0[7] in prime time and we have been maintaining that, or close to that," said Rosa Gatti, an ESPN vice president. That rating, she said, "sounds small, but that's good in cable. It's the other factors that we look at: the college-educated, high-income audience that we attract. . . . We're pleased with our growth. . . . We believe that we can maintain the all sports programming format. . . ."

ESPN has been losing money since its inception five years ago. But analysts say the network will break even by the fourth quarter of 1984 and turn a profit for the first time in 1985. Advertising revenues are projected to increase by nearly 50 percent this year to $60 million. And on Jan. 1, ESPN increased from 10 to 13 cents per subscriber the fee it charges its cable systems. In its first year ESPN charged only 4 cents and at one time even was forced to pay cable operators a small fee to entice them to carry the network. But with the increased fees and ad revenues, ESPN's economic future appears rosy. Furthermore, ABC acquired ESPN this year — for some $230 million, according to industry analysts. ABC's ownership will bring no major changes in ESPN's programming, Gatti said, but it will have an impact. "ABC will go to a site, maybe with the intent of taking up 15 minutes for 'Wide World [of Sports].' " she said. "We may be able to take an extended version of that. And ABC certainly has an extensive library of programs."

Effect of New Competition on Networks

How have declining ratings in some sports, the oversaturation of sports coverage and competition from cable affected network sports coverage? Not as drastically as one may think, said Neal Pilson, president of CBS Sports. Cable and regional pay cable sports programming do not compete directly with the networks, Pilson said. "Cable has been a supplementary business," he explained. Cable picks "up additional games, events, and packages . . . after the networks have made the initial choice. Economically, that's the way it needs to be." Pilson said that cable television still does not reach enough homes[8] to compete against the networks for the most attractive sporting events, such as the Olympics, major-league baseball and National Football League games. He predicted, moreover, that neither ESPN nor WTBS nor any other cable systems "now or in the future will have a sufficiently strong viewer base to really challenge the networks on a daily basis. . . ."

[7] A 2.0 rating indicates that 2 percent of the nation's 83.8 million television households tuned in to a particular event.

[8] According to Paul Kagan Associates, 31.75 million U.S. television households (38 percent) subscribe to cable television.

Still, Pilson said, cable has had an impact on the over-the-air networks' sports programming. Occasionally sports events on cable compete directly with network sports broadcasts, and the large number of sporting events on the dial has led to what Pilson termed an "overall dilution factor." This has resulted, he said, in a "softening of network ratings." But the networks believe this situation is temporary. "This is not in any way going to destroy us. . . . All it does is require us to manage our business in a sane fashion and to watch our costs." Pilson predicted that one way the networks will try to keep sports programming costs down is to pay less for broadcast rights.

College Football Changes

A SIGNIFICANT lowering of rights fees came this summer when the over-the-air and cable networks and syndicators signed new contracts for college football broadcast rights. From 1952 until this year, college football telecasting had been controlled by the National Collegiate Athletic Association (NCAA), the governing body of collegiate sports for some 850 colleges and universities. And until this year, the fees television paid for the right to broadcast college football games had been growing rapidly — from $16 million in 1975, for example, to $74.3 million in 1983. These costs "were growing faster than the TV package was improving," said Chuck Howard, ABC's producer of college football. "The ratings would stay flat — good, but flat — from year to year, but the cost of [obtaining] rights would shoot up 100 percent, 180 percent [in the 1960s and early 1970s]. . . . The reason we could afford to pay those incredible rights costs was that we could pass the burden along to the advertisers." [9]

The fees CBS and ABC paid for college football games this season dropped to $22 million, down from $64 million last season. The reason for the drastic decrease was a ruling by the Supreme Court on June 27 that ended the NCAA's control of televised collegiate football. The court ruled 7-2 that the NCAA's broadcast contracts with ABC, CBS and its 1983 cable contract with WTBS constituted an illegal restraint on competition, violating federal antitrust laws. [10] The ruling invali-

[9] Quoted by Ron Powers, *op. cit.*, p. 222.

[10] Justice John Paul Stevens wrote for the majority: "By restraining the quantity of television rights available for sale, the challenged practices create a limitation on output; our cases have held that such limitations are unreasonable restraints of trade."

dated 1984-85 NCAA contracts with CBS, ABC and ESPN worth more than $145 million. Individual colleges, collegiate conferences and other groups of colleges (aside from the NCAA) were free to make their own deals with network, cable and local television, and with regional and national syndicators.

In July and August various groups and individual NCAA schools signed new national contracts for the 1984 season with ABC (for $12 million), CBS ($10 million), ESPN ($9.2 million) and WTBS ($8 million). Other contracts were signed with the Public Broadcasting Service (PBS) and five syndicators. Those contracts call for the televising of 166-196 games this year. Last season only 89 were aired on ABC, CBS and WTBS. The new lineup consists of:

Network/Syndicator	Licensor	Games
ABC	College Football Association	20
CBS	Big 10 & Pac-10 Conferences; Army-Navy; Boston College-Miami (Fla.)	18
ESPN	College Football Association	15
Jefferson Productions	Atlantic Coast Conference	12
Katz Communications	Big Eight Conference; Eastern Independents	26-29
PBS	Ivy League	8
Raycom	Southwest Conference	8
SportsTime	Missouri Valley and Mid-American Conferences	16-24
TCS-Metro Sports	Big 10 & Pac-10 Conferences; 4 Notre Dame and Penn State games	31-36
	National Independent Football Network	12
WTBS	Southeastern Conference	12-14

Removing NCAA Control of TV Football

The NCAA has regulated many aspects of amateur collegiate sports since its founding in 1905. In 1951 the organization decided to regulate the televising of college games after it determined their attendance would not drop. The NCAA signed its first network contract in 1952 with NBC, and 12 games were broadcast nationally that year. For the next 25 years the NCAA signed one- and two-year exclusive contracts with the television networks, allowing the designated network to show specified games either nationally or regionally. The NCAA in 1977 signed its first four-year contract, with ABC, which had broadcast college football for the previous 11 years. From 1978 through 1981 ABC paid the NCAA an average of $30 million a year for exclusive broadcast rights to regular-season games. Then, in a break with tradition, the NCAA in May 1981 signed four-year contracts with ABC and CBS for network television and a two-year cable deal with WTBS. Meanwhile, pressure had been building to break the NCAA's monopoly on the television rights of college football — the organization did not regulate the televising of regular-season games of the other sports under its jurisdiction, nor did it regulate post-season bowl games.

Warner-Amex Cable Communications filed an unsuccessful suit against ABC and the NCAA in 1980 in federal court in Columbus, Ohio, to try to televise Ohio State University football games. In a challenge to the NCAA's jurisdiction, the College Football Association (CFA), a group of 63 major football schools formed in 1977, signed a four-year, $180 million contract with NBC in July 1981. "When the NCAA learned the CFA was considering this offer, it threatened severe sanctions — including probation and exclusion from all NCAA meets and tournaments — for any CFA member participating in the NBC plan," said Charles M. Neinas, CFA's executive director. "Facing that threat, a majority of CFA members declined the NBC offer." [11] Due to the NCAA pressure, the NBC pact was dissolved in December 1981. But the NCAA's reaction directly led to the lawsuit that resulted in the Supreme Court ruling.

The suit was filed Sept. 8, 1981, in the U.S. District Court in Oklahoma City by two of the nation's most successful collegiate football schools, the universities of Oklahoma and Georgia. A year later Judge Juan G. Burciaga ruled that the NCAA's control of college football television rights violated the 1890 Sherman Antitrust Act, which outlawed many monopolistic trade practices. Judge Burciaga concluded that the NCAA was acting as a "classic cartel" in the way it handled college football TV rights, with "an almost absolute control over the supply of college football which is made available to the networks, to television advertisers and ultimately to the viewing public...." The NCAA appealed the decision in May 1983, but the U.S. Court of Appeals for the 10th Circuit, in Denver, agreed with Judge Burciaga's ruling and the Supreme Court affirmed it.[12]

Reactions to the Supreme Court Ruling

Reaction to the Supreme Court ruling has varied greatly among the parties affected. The NCAA, as expected, condemned the decision, saying that the increased number of televised games will hurt college football attendance and provide

[11] Congressional testimony, July 31, 1984, before the House Energy and Commerce Committee's Subcommittee on Oversight and Investigations. The subcommittee was investigating the impact of the Supreme Court's decision.

[12] Two similar lawsuits, filed in September 1981 by the University of Texas at Austin and the CFA in U.S. District Court in Austin, and in August 1982 by Cox Broadcasting, ABC and NBC in Superior Court in Fulton County, Ga., were unsuccessful.

significantly less revenue to colleges, especially smaller schools that received funds from the television contracts but whose

teams rarely appear on TV. Furthermore, NCAA officials said, the competition for television dollars will influence colleges to deal with their football programs as economic entities, rather than as extracurricular activities for student-athletes. Critics argue that the big college football programs, with their multi-million-dollar scholarships and six-figure coaches' salaries, already are little more than semiprofessional operations. Ron

ESPN sportscasters Jim Simpson (left) and
Bud Wilkinson at the Rose Bowl

Powers wrote in *Supertube* that on some college teams student-athletes have "as much to do with ordinary campus life as an army of occupation has to do with the life of a conquered city."

NCAA President John L. Toner told a congressional hearing that he sees a greater effort among some major institutions to "operate football as a business . . . with possibly less than necessary regard for the educational capacity and welfare of those athletes." Charles E. Young, chancellor of the University of California at Los Angeles, agreed with that assessment. "This thrusts these programs and these institutions into the competitive forces of the American marketplace as if they are *Fortune* 500 companies. . . . This is a new, and I submit, dangerous state of affairs for intercollegiate athletics." [13]

Network and cable officials generally were pleased with the Supreme Court decision, which for the 1984 season, at least, will enable them to show more games than ever before at considerably lower cost. Rosa Gatti of ESPN, for example, characterized that network's fall college schedule as "the most attractive live college football package ever on the cable." The lower rights fees this year came about because of "multiple sellers in the marketplace," said Neal Pilson of CBS. "The price was reduced to reflect a plethora of opportunity. When supply goes up and demand is constant, price goes down."

Pilson went on to say, however, that the drop in television revenue for the colleges this year is "an abberation" because the Supreme Court decision was made about two months before the season opened. "It didn't give time for everybody to get things

---

[13] Toner and Young testified July 31, 1984, before the House Commerce Subcommittee on Oversight and Investigations.

sorted out for the rights to be negotiated and the sales to be made." In the long run, the decision will benefit colleges, Pilson said, "because many more of them will get television opportunities." He compared college football's future to college basketball's experience with television. "The total money being paid for college basketball, the total number of games being played on television, the total viewing audience [are all] the greatest in history," Pilson said.

Role of the College Football Association

While the networks have been generally pleased with the turn of events, independent local stations and some cable networks have been critical of the College Football Association. The ruling enabled the CFA to sign rights agreements. Within a month of the decision, ABC and ESPN purchased packages of games from the CFA, whose membership is made up of most of the major football powers. CFA has imposed some restrictions on the televising of these games, including limiting the number of times one team may appear on national or regional television.

The CFA contract with ABC gives that network exclusive rights to all CFA games on Saturdays from 3:30 p.m. to 7 p.m. The ESPN contract provides for exclusive CFA games from 7 p.m. to 10 p.m. The 61 CFA member schools may not sell their games to other networks during those time periods. In addition, the question of which network, if any, has the right to televise games involving a CFA team and a non-CFA team has not been ironed out.[14] "In our opinion, all that the CFA has done is just replace the NCAA," said Robert Wussler of WTBS. "It is still highly restrictive, in some instances even more restrictive" than was the NCAA.

"CFA essentially is replicating largely the behavior of the NCAA, which was found to be illegal by the Supreme Court," said Jim Hedlund, vice president for government relations for the Association of Independent Television Stations. Under previous NCAA network contracts local independents (and network affiliates) were not permitted to broadcast NCAA-member college football games. Independents believed that the Supreme Court ruling would give them opportunities to sign up games of local and regional interest. What has happened is that restrictions in CFA and several conference TV contracts severely limit the choices given to independents.

[14] The issue is now before the courts. The Pacific-10 and the Big 10 conferences have filed suit in federal court against the CFA, ABC, ESPN and the universities of Notre Dame and Nebraska over CFA's refusal to allow the UCLA-Nebraska and Southern California-Notre Dame games to be televised. Notre Dame and Nebraska are CFA members; UCLA and USC are in the Pac-10. CBS has a contract with the Big 10 and Pac-10; games involving Nebraska of the Big 8 Conference and independent Notre Dame come under the CFA's contract with ABC and ESPN.

Baseball and Pay TV

RED BARBER, the Brooklyn Dodgers radio announcer, made broadcasting history on Aug. 26, 1939, during the first game of a Dodgers-Cincinnati Reds doubleheader in Brooklyn. Sitting in the stands in the second deck at old Ebbets Field, Barber provided the play-by-play for the first televised major-league baseball game. A handful of TV receivers picked up the signal in the New York area over the NBC network. Not long after that initial experimental TV broadcast, the development of television was interrupted for nearly a decade by World War II. It wasn't until the 1947 New York Yankees-Brooklyn Dodgers World Series that baseball returned to the screen. CBS, NBC and the DuMont networks broadcast those games to an audience of only about three million. The figure was low mainly because the networks televised games only in the cities of New York, Philadelphia, Washington and Schenectady.[15] But within a few years, television spread across the nation and began attracting a huge viewing audiences.

ABC began the first regularly scheduled national series of baseball telecasts on June 6, 1953. On that day Dizzy Dean, the folksy former St. Louis Cardinals pitcher, began announcing the weekly Saturday afternoon "Game of the Week." Even though major-league baseball did not permit the weekly game to be broadcast in cities with big-league teams, the show soon became very popular. By the end of the 1953 season, Ron Powers wrote, the "Game of the Week" had "an impressive 11.4 national rating — and an even more astonishing 51 percent share of sets in use on Saturday afternoons."[16] The "Game of the Week" went to CBS in 1955, and stayed on the air until 1964.

Two decades ago organized baseball had no concerted television policy.[17] Each team was permitted to sell local or regional telecasting rights. In 1964, TV revenues ranged from the New York Yankees' $1.2 million to the estimated $300,000 taken in by the Kansas City Athletics. After the demise of the "Game of the Week" that year, the three networks provided various types of nationally televised baseball packages. NBC had begun a weekend telecast of its own in 1963, paying teams about $100,000 each for the right to broadcast the games nationally. In 1965 ABC signed a $12.2 million deal with 18 big-league clubs to broadcast games on 25 Saturdays and two holidays. Only the cities of the home and visiting teams were blacked out. The

[15] See Powers, *op. cit.*, pp. 52-64.
[16] *Ibid.*, p. 74.
[17] See "Sports on Television," *E.R.R.*, 1964 Vol. II, pp. 761-189.

Baseball's Broadcast Bonanza

Year	TV, Radio, Pay Cable Rights (in millions)	Year	TV, Radio, Pay Cable Rights (in millions)
1975	$44.5	1980	$ 80.3
1976	50.8	1981	89.5
1977	52.1	1982	118.3
1978	52.5	1983	153.6
1979	54.5	1984	267.9

Source: *Broadcasting* magazine, Feb. 27, 1984.

Yankees had a separate national TV deal that year with CBS, which owned 80 percent of the team. NBC retained control over World Series, All-Star and playoff game telecasts until 1976 when ABC signed a $94 million, four-year contract with the major leagues. The contract gave ABC rights to broadcast Monday night games, and (in alternate years) the World Series, All-Star Games and division playoffs.

Today, the 26 major-league ball clubs are still free to deal with local stations and regional pay television networks. The teams picked up some $105 million in local broadcasting rights for the 1984 season, according to *Broadcasting* magazine. As was the case 20 years ago, the Yankees led in local TV revenue ($11.7 million). The Seattle Mariners received the lowest amount ($1.4 million). The current network contract is a six-year, $1.2 billion deal signed last year with ABC and NBC. "That pact, covering the six years from 1984 through 1989, will triple network broadcast rights payments [to some $268 million] this year," *Broadcasting* noted.[18] NBC will pay some $575 million and ABC about $625 million over the six-year period.

This year NBC will have telecast 32 regular-season games (mostly on Saturday afternoons) as well as the World Series. The average 30-second commercial sells for about $35,000 on NBC's regular-season games and for $250,000 for the World Series. For its part, ABC will have carried 11 regular-season prime-time weeknight games, as well as the All-Star Game and the two best-of-five league playoff series. Thirty-second commercials on ABC weeknight games cost between $60,000 and $70,000; the top price for playoff commercials will be about $130,000 for 30 seconds.

The new contract forbids teams from airing games on local stations at the same times the nationally televised Saturday

---

[18] "New TV Contracts Push Baseball Rights to $268 Million," *Broadcasting*, Feb. 27, 1984, p. 45.

games are broadcast. "If we have an NBC game on a Saturday afternoon, none of our clubs are allowed to televise locally prior to 4 p.m., Eastern time," said Bryan Burns, director of broadcasting for major-league baseball. When NBC televises a doubleheader, which it does about four times a year, local stations are not permitted to broadcast games until after 7 p.m., Burns said. That policy has done "enormous damage to the independent stations" that carry local teams, said Jim Hedlund of the Association of Independent Television Stations.

Major-league baseball officials have voiced concerns about the large number of games broadcast by so-called "Superstations" — WTBS in Atlanta, WGN in Chicago and WOR in New York. These are local stations whose programs are carried nationwide by cable. WTBS will show 150 of the 162 Braves games this year; WGN will carry 149 Cubs games; WOR will broadcast 90 Mets contests. "It's hard for me to imagine that the Superstations exporting a game ... around the country helps anybody's attendance," Burns said.

Robert Wussler, president of WTBS, denied that cable baseball broadcasts have hurt baseball attendance or network ratings. "Major- and minor-league baseball[19] attendance have been on a steady rise," he said. Wussler added that televising nearly all of the Braves games nationally gets more people interested in the team and in baseball generally. Attendance in Atlanta has tripled since 1981, he said. Wussler credits at least part of that attendance rise to the fact that the Braves have been successful on the field. "If you put bad quality on the field and you televise it, you're not going to do your gate any good. But if you put a good team on the field and you televise it, I think you can help your team."

Big Change Wrought by Regional Pay TV

The biggest change in baseball broadcasting in recent years has been the widespread introduction of regional pay cable networks. These sports networks featuring live coverage of big-league games are offered regionally on a limited number of cable systems. This coverage is provided the viewer for a monthly fee of $8 to $12. These networks also generally broadcast professional basketball, hockey and other sports events. Five regional pay networks began operations this year, bringing to 19 the number of baseball teams that can be seen on pay cable.[20]

[19] There is no doubt that television has had an enormously negative impact on minor-league baseball. In 1949 there were 59 minor leagues with teams in more than 400 cities in the United States, Canada and Mexico. Attendance averaged about 42 million in the late 1940s. With the advent of television, the number of leagues fell to 50 in 1959, to 28 in 1969 and to 17 today. Although it has made gains in the last several years, minor-league attendance today is a shadow of what it was four decades ago. In 1983 the minors attracted 18.6 million paying customers, nearly a million more than the year before. Today 164 minor-league teams remain.

[20] The teams without pay TV contracts are: the Seattle Mariners, Cleveland Indians, Atlanta Braves, Chicago Cubs, San Francisco Giants, Oakland A's and Montreal Expos.

Regional Pay Cable Sports Networks

Network	City/State	Start-up Date
Arizona Sports Programming Network	Phoenix	Dec. 1981
Cable Sports Network	Denver	Dec. 1983
Home Sports Entertainment	Dallas	Apr. 1983
Home Sports Entertainment	Houston	Jan. 1983
Home Sports Entertainment	Pittsburgh	Apr. 1983
Home Team Sports	Baltimore-Washington, D.C.	Apr. 1984
Madison Square Garden Network	New York City	Nov. 1969
New England Sports Network	New England	Apr. 1984
ON TV*	Chicago**	May 1982
ON TV*	Los Angeles**	Apr. 1977
PRISM*	Philadelphia	Sept. 1976
Pro-Am Sports System	Michigan	Apr. 1984
RSVIP	San Diego	Apr. 1984
Sabers Network	Buffalo	Oct. 1973
Sonics Sportschannel	Seattle	Oct. 1981
Spectrum Sports	Minneapolis	Sept. 1982
Sportschannel	New England	Nov. 1981
Sports Channel	San Antonio	Oct. 1982
Sports Channel	New York City	Apr. 1979
Sports Channel	Chicago	May 1982
Sports Time Cable Network	11 Midwest states	Apr. 1984
Sports-Vue Cable Network	Milwaukee	Apr. 1984

*ON TV in Chicago and Los Angeles and PRISM broadcast movies as well as sporting events.
**Delivered via microwave STV systems.
Source: Reprinted with permission by Paul Kagan Associates Inc., from the *Pay TV Sports Newsletter*.

Although the industry still is in its early stages, analysts believe regional pay networks eventually will gain an important, if limited, share of the televised sports market. Industry sources say that to make money, regional pay networks need to sign up between 25 and 30 percent of all cable subscribers. "It's a segmented service ... that is in many cases built on two-pay or three-pay homes, meaning that [subscribers] generally will have a movie service as a foundation and sports becomes their second or third choice," said cable TV analyst Alan Cole-Ford. Those who subscribe to regional pay networks, Cole-Ford said, are in "the middle and upper reaches of the discretionary income audience, and there's a finite limit as to how well you can penetrate that [market]."

The concept of regional sports pay TV originated in 1969 when the Madison Square Garden Sports Network began operations in the New York metropolitan area. The network, which now reaches some 1.6 million households, features professional hockey, basketball and soccer, as well as some non-sports shows. Another New York area regional network, SportsChannel, went on the air in 1979, offering New York Yankees and Mets baseball games, as well as professional hockey and basketball. PRISM, one of three regional pay services that shows a nearly equal mix of sports and movies, has been in operation in the Philadelphia area since 1976. PRISM carries games of the Philadelphia professional baseball, basketball and hockey teams to some 375,000 cable viewers.

Home Team Sports (HTS), owned by Group W. Satellite Communications, is one of the regional pay networks that began operating this year. HTS, which has signed long-term contracts with the Baltimore Orioles baseball club, the Washington Bullets basketball team and the Washington Capitals hockey team, is being offered to 1.9 million cable subscribers in Maryland, Virginia, Delaware, most of North Carolina and portions of West Virginia and Pennsylvania. This year HTS will show 55 home and 25 road games of the Orioles. It also plans to broadcast college football and college basketball and other sports-related programming, including call-in shows. The remainder of its 24-hour broadcast day consists of Home Team Sports Wire, a videotex service that gives scheduling information and regional sports news. HTS and other regional pay networks also pick up each others' games to fill out their schedules.

The Future: Dividing Up the TV Spectrum

What effect has the competition from pay regional networks had on the sports coverage of cable stations, local independents and the over-the-air networks? Industry insiders concede that the new outlets represent competition for the networks. But it appears as if each of the various types of sports broadcasting is carving out its own segment of the audience. "I don't expect the regional pay networks to compete directly with the national networks," said Neal Pilson of CBS. "We have a different audience. Regional pay guys are dependent upon local fan interest.... That's a different concept than what we put on on Saturday or Sunday afternoon. We're not putting on local teams; we're putting on for the most part games with national interest." Robert Wussler of WTBS had a similar assessment. "Sure, it's competition," he said. "But ... we really do two different things. We broadcast games nationally."

Rosa Gatti of ESPN said the pay regionals "are going after a

Controlling the Game

It's no secret that television has an important voice in the scheduling of games it broadcasts, especially the big events such as the Super Bowl and World Series. The idea is to show these popular contests in prime time or on weekends to get the largest audience possible.

The performance of the Chicago Cubs this year has challenged the networks' power of scheduling. The Cubs, currently on top in the National League East, play in Wrigley Field, the only big-league park without lights. Since baseball's TV contract provides for night games in the divisional playoffs, some of the 26 owners (who share in the TV money) wanted to install temporary lights at Wrigley or move the games to a lighted stadium.

But Commissioner Bowie Kuhn ruled Aug. 30 that if the Cubs win the NL East, the first two games will be played — not at night as now scheduled — but during the day at Wrigley Field. The World Series, if the Cubs get in, will open at night in the American League city. Games 3, 4 and 5 will be held at Wrigley Field. "For once, profits and Nielsen ratings lost," *Washington Post* columnist Thomas Boswell wrote of Kuhn's decision. "Baseball won."

different [type of] event. With pay TV, you have to be willing to pay for those pay television rights. We don't even get involved in the bidding for those rights because we think is is not suitable for basic cable." Another factor, Gatti said, is the fact that cable subscribers do not have to pay extra monthly fees to receive ESPN. "They may not want to pay that extra $10 or $20," she said. "And they may say, 'Well, I want to watch sports, but I'm not going to pay for it.' They'll turn to ESPN." Local independents are more concerned with competition from the networks than with the impact of regional pay networks.

In sum, sports broadcasting is experiencing what Alan Cole-Ford termed an "evolution in the distribution sequence." This evolution, he said, can be compared to what has happened with movies in the last decade with the rapidly growing popularity of pay TV and videocassette recorders. "Sequential distribution shuffles itself to accommodate all those outlets," Cole-Ford said. In the case of sports broadcasting, it is predicted that the biggest professional sports contests will continue on the over-the-air networks, that the regional pay networks will show college and professional events of interest to local audiences, and that the cable networks and local independents will fill in with prime-time and weekend events the networks do not choose to televise. "Sports will continue to be an important part of television," Jim Zrake of the USA Network predicted. "It's live television; it's exciting; it's escapism. It's all the things that people enjoy."

Selected Bibliography

Books

Barber, Red, *The Broadcasters*, Dial Press, 1970.
Barnouw, Eric, *Tube of Plenty: The Evolution of American Television*, Oxford University Press, 1975.
Durso, Joseph, *The All-American Dollar: The Big Business of Sports*, Houghton Mifflin, 1971.
Lasch, Christopher, *The Culture of Narcissism: American Life in an Age of Diminishing Expectations*, Norton, 1978.
Novak, Michael, *The Joy of Sports: End Zones, Bases, Baskets, Balls, and the Consecration of the American Spirit*, Basic Books, 1976.
Patton, Phil, *Razzle-Dazzle: The Curious Marriage of Television and Professional Football*, Dial, 1984.
Powers, Ron, *Supertube: The Rise of Television Sports*, Coward-McGann, 1984
Wicklein, John, *Electronic Nightmare*, Viking, 1981.

Articles

Broadcasting, selected issues.
Cable Television Business, selected issues.
CableVision, selected issues.
Frank, Allan Dodds, "The USFL Meets the Sophomore Jinx," *Forbes*, Feb. 13, 1984.
Gerlach, Larry, "Telecommunications and Sports," *Vital Speeches of the Day*, March 15, 1984.
Pay TV Sports (published by Paul Kagan Associates), selected issues.
Taaffe, William, "The Dawn of a New Era," *Sports Illustrated*, April 2, 1984.
"The NCAA's Goal-Line Stand on TV Rights," *Business Week*, April 9, 1984.
Vance, N. Scott, "NCAA Weighs Plan to Divvy Up Money from a TV-Rich Basketball Tournament," *The Chronicle of Higher Education*, Feb. 29, 1984.

Reports and Studies

Editorial Research Reports: "Cable TV's Future," 1982 Vol. II, p. 717; "Television in the Eighties," 1980 Vol. I, p. 325; "Sports on Television," 1964 Vol. II, p. 763.
National Cable Television Association, "Cable Television Developments," June 1984; "Satellite Services Report," May 1984.

Graphics: cover illustration by Staff Artist Robert Redding: photo p. 72 by ESPN.

HISTORIC PRESERVATION

by

Robert Benenson

**Feb. 10
1 9 8 4**

Editor's Note: Rhodes Tavern, the Washington, D.C., building that was the subject of a long battle between preservationists and developers *(see p. 99)*, was torn down on Sept. 10, 1984. An initiative approved by District voters that might have saved the building was declared unconstitutional by the city's Superior Court., and the Supreme Court refused to intervene, clearing the way for the demolition.

HISTORIC PRESERVATION

P RESERVATION of buildings and other structures of historic, cultural or architectural significance has taken on a new importance in most American cities. This was amply illustrated in Washington, D.C., in 1983. In June Congress decided to spend $49 million to restore the last original wall of the U.S. Capitol — the West Front — rather than destroy it to build a $70 million extension to the building. In September the Old Post Office building, a steepled landmark built in 1899, was reopened with fanfare as a retail-entertainment-office complex. October brought the opening of a controversial office building that retained the facades of the townhouses which had long occupied the site. And in November the fight to save the run-down building that once housed Rhodes Tavern, Washington's first City Hall, culminated in a citywide referendum.

Long derided as eccentrics, preservationists have carved out an influential role in national, state and local decision-making. Spurred by what they regarded as the ravages of "bulldozer" urban renewal programs, preservation activists have gone from small ad hoc constituencies to a broad public base of support. "As the United States has grown and matured, so has its stock of buildings," wrote Grace Anderson in the June 1982 issue of *Architectural Record*. "And people looking at these buildings, both architects and laymen, want to save them — sometimes for esthetic reasons, sometimes for historical reasons, most often, perhaps, out of a loathing for waste." [1]

While today's preservationists fight, as did their predecessors, to save historic houses and individual landmarks, their emphasis has shifted to the use of old commercial buildings in programs of economic development and neighborhood revitalization. The most publicized trend has been the conversion of factories, public buildings and markets to popular shopping and entertainment complexes: Washington's Old Post Office is a prime example. Thousands of other buildings have been restored to their original grandeur or converted for new uses. Declining neighborhoods in cities across the country have been revived through the housing rehabilitation efforts of neighborhood groups or "urban pioneers."

---

[1] "Renovated Buildings Find New Purpose," *Architectural Record*, June 1982, p. 81.

Through the efforts of the National Trust for Historic Preservation *(see p. 91)*, lobbying groups like Washington's Preservation Action and hundreds of state and local organizations, preservationists have garnered government funding and protections for "the built environment." [2] The cause does not have universal appeal, however. Many developers still view preservationists as anti-progress — and anti-profit — obstructionists. Advocates for the poor take a jaundiced view of "gentrifiers" whose neighborhood revitalization projects often displace low-income residents. And after experiencing a decade of increasing federal support, the preservation movement finds itself fighting off Reagan administration attempts to cut funding and roll back some protections.

Changing Emphasis of Preservationism

The early preservation movement in the United States concerned itself with saving buildings primarily of historic importance. The first recorded preservation action was the 1816 purchase by the city of Philadelphia of Independence Hall — site of the signing of the Declaration of Independence — from the state of Pennsylvania. The successful campaign waged from 1853 to 1859 by the Mount Vernon Ladies Association to save George Washington's Virginia estate was the first nationwide preservation drive, and it provided a model for the Colonial Dames of America, the Daughters of the American Revolution, and other "patriotic" organizations that became involved in preservation in the late 19th and early 20th centuries. "The preservation movement was prompted by intangible or associative reasons, someone famous slept there, or a famous battle occurred," said Mary Means, National Trust vice president for program development.[3]

Gradually, changing architectural styles, especially in cities, sparked interest in preserving buildings that were not necessarily commemorative in nature. Citizens' groups and some city governments concluded that buildings of more mundane origin should be protected, either because a certain architectural style was closely linked with the city's past or because architectural variety made the city a more interesting place to live or visit.

These early efforts were especially successful in cities where economic decline had kept historic areas, usually low-income neighborhoods, relatively free of development pressure. Charleston, S.C., created the first "historic district" in 1924; New Orleans followed by protecting the Vieux Carré (the

---

[2] The National Trust for Historic Preservation will be referred to in the following pages as the "National Trust" or the "Trust."

[3] Unless otherwise noted, Means and others quoted in this report were interviewed by the author.

Among the first American preservation efforts: Philadelphia's Independence Hall, top left; a street in New Orleans' French Quarter, top right; and George Washington's home, Mount Vernon, bottom.

French Quarter) in 1936. Development and alterations to architectural details were strictly controlled in these areas.

This was not the case in cities where downtown development replaced well-known landmarks with skyscraping steel-and-glass towers and other structures that provided more profit for the property owners and more tax revenue for the cities. Many of today's preservation activists cut their teeth in the losing efforts to save structures such as New York's Pennsylvania Station, torn down in 1963 to make way for the new Madison Square Garden arena and an office building, and the Chicago Stock Exchange, razed in 1972 and replaced by an office tower.

Preservationists blame post-World-War-II federal policies for the loss of neighborhoods important to the history and social fabric of many cities. Federal tax laws that allowed write-offs for the costs of demolition discouraged rehabilitation and en-

85

couraged destruction of old but salvageable properties. Federal mortgage subsidies geared to suburban development created incentives for middle-class taxpayers to leave the city behind. Thousands of urban buildings in disrepair were toppled in the name of "slum clearance" or "economic development."

The fledgling preservation movement took a defensive posture during this period. "We spent most of our early years standing in front of bulldozers after the demolition permits had been let," said Nelly Longsworth, president of Preservation Action.[4] Preservationists also suffered from their image in popular culture as a group of "blue-haired" upper-class women and eccentric "little old ladies in tennis shoes."

The activism of these groups, however, set the stage for the advances of the past two decades. In 1966, Congress passed the Historic Preservation Act, which created the Advisory Council on Historic Preservation and set up other programs that vastly increased the government's role in preservation *(see p. 91)*. In ensuing years preservationists became eligible for money from a variety of federal housing and urban renewal programs, as well as grant and loan programs administered by the National Trust. Small tax breaks in the 1976 Tax Reform Act for rehabilitation of historic structures were expanded significantly in 1981 *(see p. 92)*.

These financial incentives, combined with the success of preservation-oriented commercial projects, helped modify developers' dire views of preservation. Old buildings converted to shopping or entertainment complexes revived dying downtown areas *(see p. 87)*. Cities such as Savannah, Ga., used their architectural heritage to boost tourism. Restoration of valuable but decaying housing stock not only revitalized old neighborhoods, but turned some of them — Philadelphia's Society Hill and New York's Brooklyn Heights, for example — into fashionable and expensive places to live. The new-found profitability of preservation drew in real estate, investment and development interests that had been traditional antagonists of the movement. "There has been such money poured in, invested in preservation on such a large scale now, that when the developers start doing it, we've lost the final vestige of 'blue-hair' association," said Mary Means.

Key Element in Urban Planning Process

Although there are still some bitter battles when development and preservation goals clash *(see p. 98)*, preservation is now regarded as a legitimate and, in many cities, a key element in

---

[4] Described by Longsworth as a grass-roots lobby, Preservation Action was founded in 1975 to monitor and promote preservation-oriented legislation in Congress. The organization's activities are sustained by membership fees and corporate funding.

urban planning. Over 900 cities have established landmarks preservation commissions. In some communities these panels are restricted to putting up plaques on buildings and monuments regarded as landmarks. But in others the commissions are quasi-legal and can block the demolition of designated structures, despite the wishes of the buildings' owners.

The right of cities to control development through landmarks commissions was established by the U.S. Supreme Court in 1978. Spurred by a protest movement led by Jacqueline Kennedy Onassis, New York City's Landmarks Preservation Commission denied a request by the Penn Central Transportation Co. to build a 53-story office building atop the landmark Grand Central Terminal, which it owned. Because the terminal site was zoned for taller buildings, Penn Central sued the city, charging that its "air rights" over the terminal were confiscated in violation of the Fifth Amendment, which bars the taking of private property for public use "without just compensation." The Supreme Court ruled 6-3 against Penn Central.[5]

Several cities have integrated preservation into their "master plans" for development. In November 1982 Denver passed a new zoning law for its 23-block Lower Downtown area that provides economic incentives for development of residential housing and preservation of the district's turn-of-the-century commercial buildings and warehouses. Efforts to stem the "Manhattanization" of downtown San Francisco led to a zoning proposal that would preserve 271 historic buildings, create incentives to save 223 other buildings, and reduce the height limitation on skyscrapers from 700 to 550 feet. To compensate building owners and developers, the Denver and San Francisco plans both contain "development rights transfer" provisions, which allow owners of landmark buildings to sell their unused size potential to developers of other properties, who can then build structures bigger than allowed under the zoning laws *(see box, p. 93)*.

Popularity of Commercial Renovation

In 1967, a group of Denver preservationists completed the rehabilitation of several blocks of small Victorian commercial buildings — restoring the facades to their original appearances while remodeling the interiors along the patterns of suburban shopping centers. The Larimer Square project, aimed at drawing tourists and shoppers back into Denver's depressed downtown community, thrived and quickly was copied in other cities. Conversion of San Francisco's Ghirardelli chocolate factory into

---

[5] *Penn Central Transportation Co. v. City of New York*, 438 U.S. 104 (1978).

such a complex was completed in 1968. Salt Lake City's Trolley Square (1972) was a converted trolley barn; Akron's Quaker Square (1975) was a converted Quaker Oats cereal factory.

These early examples of "adaptive reuse" or "commercial rehabilitation" have been overshadowed by their much larger and more glamorous progeny. In 1976 developer James Rouse completed work on the conversion of Boston's Faneuil Hall, a famed Revolutionary-era meeting place, and the Quincy Markets into a 365,000-square-foot shopping-entertainment complex that now draws 12 million visitors a year. Rouse also designed the Grand Avenue Mall (1981), a Victorian-style arcade that is drawing shoppers back to downtown Milwaukee.

His biggest project opened last July: the South Street Seaport in lower Manhattan. Three blocks of deteriorating 19th-century Federal-style commercial buildings near the Fulton Fish Market and adjacent to the Wall Street financial district have been spruced up and their storefronts filled with fashionable boutiques, speciality shops and restaurants ranging from fast-food to nouvelle cuisine. A three-story mall, designed to fit in with surrounding architecture, also was constructed.

The success of such projects has sparked a virtual industry. In addition to Washington's Old Post Office building, similar projects are under way or have been completed in a pair of 1904 tobacco warehouses in Durham, N.C., and in abandoned breweries in Baton Rouge, La. (1891) and Denver (1863). The proliferation of the concept concerns some preservationists. "Are we creating a preservation style ... the 'Rousification' [of historic buildings]?" asked Mary Means of the National Trust, a founding member of Don't Tear It Down, the coalition that saved the Old Post Office from demolition. "I had very mixed emotions on seeing that development in there, because I thought to myself, am I in HarborPlace,[6] am I in Boston, am I in Ghirardelli Square? Is this what preservation has done, [created] a little bit nicer shopping center?" But Means amended her comments by noting that the Old Post Office building, so recently decaying and near-abandoned, "has people in it again."

Others involved in preservation note that these well-publicized projects are just a small segment of the "adaptive use" market. There are a number of other purposes to which adaptive reuse has been put. One popular trend has been the conversion of old public or industrial buildings into apartments. The

---

[6] HarborPlace, a shopping-entertainment-office complex at the Inner Harbor in downtown Baltimore, was a Rouse project commissioned after the Faneuil Hall success in Boston. Although similar in style to other such projects, HarborPlace is primarily new construction, an example of urban renewal rather than preservation.

Boston's Quincy Markets as they once were and after 1976 conversion into shopping and restaurant complex.

building that once housed the Beekman Downtown Hospital near the South Street Seaport complex in New York has been converted to the Seaport Park Condominiums; its 26 units range in price from $175,000 to $625,000. A Blatz brewery in Milwaukee is being converted into 146 apartments.

Schools are also popular for adaptive reuse projects. Seattle hoped to raise $1.2 million in revenue in 1983 from the lease of 20 historic school buildings for conversion into condominiums, art centers, stores and other kinds of educational institutions. A school built in Salem, Va., in 1912 has been turned into a new City Hall while in Boston a vacant gas company warehouse and garage has been converted into Jamaica Plain High School.

Mark Weinheimer, director of financial services at the National Trust, also pointed out that much of the preservation activity is aimed at continued, not adaptive, use — "fixing up old office buildings to be new office buildings, or old hotels to be new hotels." A number of famous but declining hotels have been restored to their original grandeur by developers — among them the Adolphus in Dallas, the Lancaster in Houston and the Seelbach in Louisville. Abandoned movie theatres have been

Restored downtown street in Madison, Ind.

modified into performing arts centers in Cleveland, Richmond, Memphis, Dallas, Winston-Salem, N.C., and Jacksonville, Fla.

Efforts to Revive Main Street America

Commercial rehabilitation efforts are not restricted to big cities. Many smaller communities are attempting to resuscitate their once-thriving "Main Streets." These downtown commercial centers declined in the post-World-War-II era as middle-class shoppers gravitated to the highway "strip" and the suburban shopping mall. In their efforts to modernize, downtown shop owners turned to aluminum siding and other false fronts, covering up the distinctive Main Street look and destroying the architectural unity of their areas.

The major impetus for downtown revival has come from the Main Street program sponsored by the National Trust, which has provided assistance for planning and financing revitalization projects to 30 communities — five each in Colorado, Georgia, Massachusetts, North Carolina, Pennsylvania and Texas — with populations ranging from 1,400 to 49,000.[7] According to Means, who ran the Main Street Center until her recent promotion to vice president, the program illustrates the new pragmatism in preservation philosophy. "We want to save the buildings, we'd like to see them painted and beautifully restored, but you're not going to be able to afford the second coat of paint if the economic engine can't buy it," said Means. Means added that the Main Street Center advises town planners not to compete directly with the massive and impersonal suburban shopping malls but to provide an alternative. "The niche is to try to be the best Main Street you can, using the buildings and the ambiance and the personal service as assets to build an entire strategy for revitalization," she said.

---

[7] The experimental Main Street Project established in 1977 became the National Trust's Main Street Center in 1980.

According to Means, in just three years the project produced $60 million in new investment and 400 new jobs in the 30 towns and cities. The successes, which have spurred many imitators, were beyond the expectations of the program designers. "Never in a million years would I have thought we could put our finger into something and come out with a plum like this," Means said. "The economic development people jumped on the bandwagon, the traditional planners, it's brought a constituency together that formerly was at war with one another."

Support Programs

FEDERAL INTEREST in historic preservation is comparatively recent. The federal government took its first official notice of preservation in the 1930s. In 1933, the National Park Service was authorized to coordinate the Historic American Building Survey (HABS); over the past 50 years, measured drawings, photographs and written material on over 16,000 buildings have been recorded under HABS.[8] The Historic Sites Act of 1935 created the National Register of Historic Places, a listing of important landmarks. Over the years, the National Park Service has also been authorized to purchase or maintain hundreds of historic landmarks, many of which have been restored and are open to the public.

Congress chartered the National Trust for Historic Preservation in 1949 to provide a central national focus for preservation activities and to serve as an information clearinghouse and coordinator of national preservation conferences. Although the trust has received federal funding since its inception, including $4.5 million in fiscal year 1984, it is a private organization that relies on corporate grants and membership dues for much of its financing. Since its creation the trust has provided technical assistance and an influential voice to struggling local preservation groups. But only since the early 1970s has it provided direct financial aid to preservation projects.

Its first assistance program was the National Preservation Revolving Fund, established in 1971. Modeled after similar programs run by local organizations, the revolving fund is essentially a money-recycling plan. The fund provides loans or loan guarantees to organizations and individuals to purchase and

---

[8] Since 1934, the Library of Congress and the American Institute of Architects (AIA) have been partners with the National Park Service on HABS. A similar program, the Historic American Engineering Record, was established in 1969 to record examples of outdated technology. Participants include the National Park Service, the Library of Congress and the American Society of Civil Engineers.

rehabilitate historic properties. When work is completed, the properties are sold with covenants to guarantee that the new owners will protect the historic qualities. The proceeds from such sales are used to pay off the loans, with the money returning to the revolving fund to be used on other projects.

At present, the National Trust conducts four other financial assistance programs. The Endangered Properties Fund provides grants and loans for the maintenance or purchase of historic properties in danger of being lost to demolition or neglect. The Critical Issues Fund provides grants to cities and preservation organizations to study the feasibility of preservation plans and to head off brewing controversies. The Preservation Services Fund provides small grants, generally under $4,000, to enable organizations to obtain consultant services and set up preservation education programs.

The final program, the Inner-City Ventures Fund, was created in 1981 as a response to concerns that "neighborhood preservation" was displacing poor residents *(see p. 96)*. The fund provides grants and loans on a matching basis to neighborhood organizations for the rehabilitation of low-income housing. The local groups must come up with $5 for every $1 provided by the trust. According to program coordinator Mark Weinheimer, the 22 groups assisted to date have averaged $16 in local money for every trust dollar.

Federal Assistance and Tax Incentives

Aside from the National Park Service programs and the money appropriated to the National Trust, Congress has been reluctant to create funding programs specifically for preservation. Money has been available, however, through various development or housing assistance programs, most of which are administered by the Department of Housing and Urban Development (HUD). Urban Development Action Grant program funds were used in the Grand Avenue Mall in Milwaukee, the South Street Seaport in New York, and the conversion of a courthouse into a performing arts center in Cambridge, Mass. The availability of Community Development Block Grant (CDBG) funds for neighborhood development varies because the cities control the apportionment of the lump-sum federal assistance. Mark Weinheimer cited Cincinnati and Pittsburgh as cities that fund preservation projects with CDBG money, but he said, "Other cities won't give a dime to neighborhood groups or projects; most are somewhere in between."

Under the "urban homesteading" program, established in the 1960s and active in over 100 cities, HUD-owned vacant or abandoned houses are given to cities, which sell them to urban

Development Rights

Liberal size limits written into most city zoning laws over the last half-century have spurred the construction of tall buildings in downtown areas. While most new buildings are as tall as the law permits, many older buildings are often shorter than they could be under the law. Looked at another way, a three-story building in a district zoned for 50-story buildings has 47 stories of unused potential.

For a property owner or developer who sees such situations in strictly dollars-and-cents terms, the potential for increased revenue creates a strong incentive to raze the smaller building and replace it with an office tower. At the same time, preservationists, often with the cooperation of city landmarks commissions, want to save many of the older buildings.

Thus a city may be caught between two seemingly contradictory goals: the need for job-creating, revenue-producing development and the desire to preserve its architectural heritage. One solution being explored in several cities is the transfer of development rights. The owner of a landmark building in a high-rise zone may sell the rights to develop its unused potential — the difference between the size limit and the actual size of the building — to the developer of another property. The potential is then applied to the purchaser's property, which is allowed to exceed the size limit.

Washington is one city where transfer of development rights is practiced. In 1976, the owners of the Christian Heurich mansion (1894), located in a burgeoning downtown area, sold its development rights to the developer of a nearby office building. The sale provided a $4.5 million endowment for the maintenance of the older building. "I think it saved the character of that particular part of the city," said Preservation Action President Nelly Longsworth.

The strategy is not without its opponents. In *The New York Times* October 1, architecture critic Paul Goldberger wrote that development rights transfer "can make for an even denser midtown, just at a time when public concern over the building boom of recent years has led to calls to slow down construction somewhat."

pioneers for as little as $1. The purchasers are required to rehabilitate the houses and live in them for at least three years. HUD also provides low-interest loans to rehabilitate single-family, multifamily and mixed-use housing.[9] The Federal Housing Administration has a variety of loan and mortgage insurance programs aimed at housing rehabilitation.

---

[9] Interest rates are 3 percent for borrowers with incomes less than 80 percent of the local median, 9 percent for other borrowers.

The impact of these funding programs has been minor compared with the boost provided by tax incentives written into the law in recent years. Building upon smaller incentives provided by the 1976 Tax Reform Act, the 1981 Economic Recovery Tax Act allowed a 25 percent tax credit for rehabilitation of historic, income-producing properties. According to Ian Spatz of the National Trust, "What the 25 percent incentive finally did was to even the score, and the score ... was biased toward new construction because of the faster write-off periods that you can get on depreciation."

Only buildings listed on the National Register of Historic Places are eligible for the 25 percent tax credit, and the owners of even these buildings must go through a certification process administered by the Technical Preservation Services (TPS), a division of the National Park Service.[10] Applications for certification are filed with the state historic preservation offices, which filter out those that are obviously ineligible for the tax benefit.[11] The rest are forwarded to the regional offices of the National Park Service. TPS Director Ward Jandl estimated that about half of the proposals for certification are modified in negotiations with developers. About 8 percent of the projects are ultimately denied certification.

The tax incentives have sparked a boom in the utilization of historic buildings for commercial, industrial or housing purposes. According to the National Park Service, 2,572 projects were certified in fiscal 1983 for an aggregate investment of more than $2.6 billion, a 43 percent increase over fiscal 1982. "The tax incentives have been spectacularly successful," said Spatz. "What it did was to advertise preservation to a group that never thought of themselves as preservationists, whose primary motivation was not a desire to save the American heritage ... people who were looking for an opportunity in the real estate area."

One aspect of the tax credit is causing some anxiety on Capitol Hill, however. The sale-leaseback provisions of the 1981 tax law allow non-profit organizations to sell their historic buildings to private investors, who would thus be eligible for the tax credit and who would, in turn, lease the facility back to the original non-profit owner. Most of the controversy surrounded

---

[10] A tax credit of 20 percent is available to owners of buildings more than 40 years old that are ineligible for the higher credit. A 15 percent tax credit is available for buildings between 30 and 40 years old. Federal tax laws also regard the donation of most property "easements" to non-profit preservation organizations as deductible charitable contributions. Historic-property owners uninterested in the tax advantages may sell their easements for profit.

[11] The creation of the state historic preservation offices was mandated by the 1966 Historic Preservation Act. Along with their tax certification roles, these offices also conduct preservation programs and are responsible for nomination of properties within their states to the National Register.

the efforts of Hartford, Conn., to literally "sell City Hall." Bills by Sen. Robert Dole, R-Kan., and Rep. J. J. Pickle, D-Texas, to close or tighten this loophole languished in Congress during the 1983 session, but could be considered again this year.

Advisory Council as Federal Watchdog

Not all federal preservation actions have to do with money. In response to the outcry over the effect of the federal urban renewal and highway building projects on historic properties, Congress created, as part of the 1966 Historic Preservation Act, the Advisory Council on Historic Preservation. Section 106 of the act requires that any project using federal funds or operating under federal license must "take into account the effect of the undertaking on any district, site, building, structure or object that is included in or eligible for inclusion on the National Register." The law also requires that the Advisory Council be given opportunity to comment on the proposed project.

If the council finds that a project will harm historic properties, it will attempt to negotiate with the federal agency with jurisdiction over the project to remedy the deleterious effects. The council has no enforcement or judicial functions; if the agency in charge is determined to go ahead with the project, it can do so. However, the council occasionally has joined with activists in efforts to block or amend projects. In the mid-1970s, the council fought successfully to reroute an extension of Interstate 83 through Baltimore, which would have wiped out the historic Fells Point neighborhood as well as the site of HarborPlace.

While preservationists back the council's efforts, members of the Reagan administration view many of its actions as examples of the kind of excessive regulation they are committed to reduce. In a letter to Advisory Council Chairman Alexander Aldrich last September, Secretary of the Interior James G. Watt called the Section 106 regulations "exceptionally objectional, placing . . . needless requirements on federal agencies and state and local governments." In each of its last three budgets, the administration has attempted to reduce financing for the Advisory Council and eliminate federal funding altogether for the National Trust and the state preservation offices. To date, Congress has rejected these budget-cutting requests.

Signs of Backlash

WHILE the preservation movement has made significant gains, preservationists themselves admit to some negative results. The popularity of adapting old industrial buildings into housing has led to what is known as "gut renovation" — the historic exteriors are left intact, but the insides of the building are totally remodeled. "It is an ironic consequence of the present public awareness of older buildings that a wholesale destruction of their interiors is sweeping [New York City]," wrote Arnold L. Markowitz in *Metropolis* magazine. "While allegedly preserving and recycling our building stock, gut renovators are destroying it from within as surely as did the bulldozers of the urban renewal days of the 1950s and 1960s."

Another controversial trend has been the integration of old building facades into new buildings. As a compromise with a group of activists, The George Washington University in Washington, D.C., agreed to preserve the facades of the town houses it was razing to make way for a new office building on "Red Lion Row." However, some preservationists opposed the concept and, after viewing the results upon completion last October, the execution. "That's really sort of pitiful to see that sort of thing happening," said Preservation Action President Nelly Longsworth. "That doesn't seem to be historic preservation at all."

An August editorial in *Preservation News* stated that "facade-ectomy" was a compromise that preservationists should not accept. "While many developers have been enlightened to preservation's benefits," the editorial continued, "there are some left who simply want to exploit the current popularity of old buildings." [12]

Gentrification: Displacement of the Poor

One of the most controversial aspects of preservation occurs when middle- and upper-middle-class people buy and rehabilitate old houses in declining neighborhoods. They claim their "neighborhood revitalization" efforts upgrade the community

---

[12] *Preservation News* is a monthly publication of the National Trust.

and benefit the entire city. But low-income residents displaced by the restoration criticize the process as "gentrification."

Restoration of these older neighborhoods occurred on a broad scale in many cities in the 1960s and 1970s as homeowners, many of whom had long before deserted the city for the suburbs, discovered the architectural and structural value of old houses. According to Everett Ortner, a prominent urban pioneer, the traditional American philosophy of "new is good" and "bad is old" is especially wrong when it comes to housing. "The old houses were built of very-high quality, especially 19th-century urban housing," said Ortner. "Today we build junk."

When the movement began, property values in these areas were depressed. Ortner said that "a person could buy a wonderful house on a schoolteacher's salary [and] live like a millionaire." However, the success stories and disenchantment with suburban living created a demand that sent prices and property taxes soaring and often forced longtime residents to seek more affordable housing. A paper released by the National Trust in 1977 noted "well-above-average to extraordinary residential property value levels ... in all urban historic districts canvassed." [13] *The New York Times* recently reported that restored town houses in Greenwich Village were going for as much as $700,000, in Brooklyn Heights for $650,000.[14]

Gentrification has made many low-income urbanites suspicious of the preservation process. In early 1983, when preservationists attempted to extend the Dupont Circle historic district in Washington, D.C., into the low-income, mainly black Shaw area, a Shaw community leader called it "a land-grab by the middle- and upper-middle-class Caucasians that live around Dupont Circle." Community groups in the Over-the-Rhine community in Cincinnati, where 37 percent of the inhabitants are below the poverty line, unsuccessfully opposed the listing of the neighborhood in the National Register.

Many preservationists say they are not to blame for the displacement that occurs as a result of neighborhood revitalization activities. "I'm getting tired of preservation taking it on the nose as the great displacer," said Mary Means of the National Trust. An editorial in *Preservation News* last July commented, "If society believes that displacement is bad and decent housing is necessary, it must be willing to make ... commitments — both in the public and private sectors — to provide hope and a better life for the inner-city poor."

[13] "Values of Residential Properties in Urban Historic Districts: Georgetown, Washington, D.C. and Other Selected Districts," National Trust for Historic Preservation, 1977.
[14] *The New York Times*, Oct. 29, 1983.

Other preservationists point to the number of rehabilitation projects directed at low-income people. According to the National Park Service, over half of the housing units created under the tax-credit program were for low- and moderate-income families. Mark Weinheimer said the National Trust's Inner-City Ventures Fund program supports non-profit neighborhood organizations that are "trying to preserve neighborhood fabric, fighting displacement, fighting gentrification." The purpose of the program, Weinheimer said, ". . . is to show that preservation is a good positive tool, not something to be feared by low-income individuals. . . ."

Conflicts With Developers Still Common

Low-income persons are not the only urbanites opposed to landmark designation. Private property owners and developers have attempted to block designation of many buildings, especially in cities with strong legal prohibitions against demolition or alteration of designated properties. For example, Broadway theater owners in New York City oppose landmark designation; the fear is that if a theater someday becomes unprofitable to run as a theater, its owner will be unable to sell, adapt or demolish the landmark and will thus be stuck with a money-losing proposition.

Many churches are trying to escape from landmark designation as well. The board of directors of St. Bartholomew's Episcopal Church, located in an area of high property values on Park Avenue in New York, is fighting to have the landmark designation of its parish house lifted so that it can be razed to make way for a 59-story office building. Church leaders argue that the landmark designation impinges on the church's constitutionally protected freedom of religion; they say the church will use part of the proceeds from the office building for its work with the poor. The matter is before the city's Landmarks Preservation Commission, which must take action before the end of May. A bill to exempt churches from landmark laws is expected to be

Far left, Rhodes Tavern when it was Washington's first City Hall. Middle, the building as it looked in 1983. Left, an artist's conception of how the restored building might be fit into the new Metropolitan Square complex.

considered by the New York state Legislature in its 1984 session.

Another example of the controversy that can arise when a citizens' or preservation group tries to block demolition of a historic or locally cherished landmark is occuring in the nation's capital. The Rhodes Tavern building (1800) in downtown Washington stands in the way of the completion of the $100 million office-retail Metropolitan Square complex. A six-year fight by the Save Historic Rhodes Tavern Committee, led by former government lawyer Joseph N. Grano Jr., was put before the city's voters last November.

Preservation forces said that the building should be incorporated into the development plans and restored as a tourist attraction. But developer Oliver T. Carr argued that the building is of little historic importance and complained that delays resulting from the preservation fight had cost him over $1 million. The initiative, which called for the creation of a commission to determine how to save the vacant and rundown building, passed by a 60-40 margin.

Unlike many other issues, there is a rift in opinion among preservationists over the Rhodes Tavern battle. Speaking for herself and not in her capacity as National Trust vice president, Mary Means described the Rhodes Tavern battle as "a mountain out of a molehill" which could hurt preservationism. "Now we're beginning to get a backlash, because preservation is trying to save everything," Means said. "We've got to start looking at it as the management of change and not the prevention of change."

Selected Bibliography

Books

Hosmer, Charles B. Jr., *Preservation Comes of Age: From Williamsburg to the National Trust, 1926-1949,* University Press of Virginia for the National Trust for Historic Preservation, 1981.

Reed, Richard Ernie, *Return to the City,* Doubleday, 1979.

Weinberg, Nathan, *Preservation in American Towns and Cities,* Westview, 1979.

Wrenn, Tony P. and Elizabeth D. Mulloy, *America's Forgotten Architecture,* National Trust for Historic Preservation, 1976.

Articles

Anderson, Grace, "Renovated Buildings Find New Purpose," *Architectural Record,* June 1982.

Collins, Richard C., "Changing Views on Historical Conservation in Cities," *The Annals of the American Academy of Political and Social Science,* September 1980.

Malanowski, Jamie, "Broadway Cacophony," *The Atlantic,* November 1983.

Reed, J. D., "Capital Success in Washington," *Time,* Oct. 17, 1983.

Russell, Stephanie, "When Campus and Community Collide," *Historic Preservation,* September-October 1983.

Von Eckardt, Wolf, "Saving the Unfashionable Past," *Time,* Feb. 21, 1983.

Wiessler, David, "When Developers Bump Up Against Tradition," *U.S. News & World Report,* July 26, 1982.

Reports and Studies

Advisory Council on Historic Preservation, "Report to the President and the Congress of the United States," 1982.

National Trust for Historic Preservation, "Financial Assistance Programs," 1982.

Graphics: Cover illustration and p. 95 art by staff artist Belle Burkhart; p. 85 Independence Hall photo courtesy of Independence National Historical Park, Mount Vernon photo courtesy of Mount Vernon Ladies Assn., New Orleans photo courtesy of Greater New Orleans Tourist and Convention Commission, Inc.; p. 89 photos courtesy of The Rouse Co.; p. 90 photo courtesy of the National Trust for Historic Preservation; pp. 98-99 photos courtesy of Save Historic Rhodes Tavern Committee; p. 99 conception by artist Tom Kozar.

THE WORLD OF FASHION

by

Robert Benenson

**Mar. 22
1 9 8 5**

THE WORLD OF FASHION

FASHION IS not dead. Only a decade ago it was fashionable, so to speak, to predict that the dictates of haute couture designers would be swept aside by blue-jean-clad masses insistent on "doing their own thing." Instead, as the baby-boomers moved from the classroom toward the board room, they were swept up in the "dress for success" movement. And as the Pepsi generation became the Yuppie generation, many of its members began to pursue clean-cut style with a vengeance.

The survival of fashion does not mean its world is unchanged. American women no longer adapt their tastes or distort their bodies in response to the biannual pronouncements of Paris couturiers.[1] European haute couture has been making a comeback in the last few years, aided by the strong American dollar. But there are no fashion dictators today — no Chanel, no Dior — to lay down the law on cut or hemline length. Most couturiers now support their high-fashion activities with ready-to-wear lines. All eyes no longer turn to Paris for the latest styles, either; Milan, London and Tokyo also have emerged as fashion centers.

Foreign design is no longer the focus for many American women anyway. They have come to rely on home-grown talents — Calvin Klein, Geoffrey Beene, Bill Blass and Liz Claiborne, to name a few — for fashion direction. While the top designers still have their exclusive and expensive lines, most have produced moderately priced lines to meet the needs and demands of style-conscious working women. One of the most significant events in this trend was the decision by high-society designer Halston to create a line for the J. C. Penney chain. While some industry analysts hail the new availability of fashions for the masses, others worry about an over-saturation of designer products that could cause them to lose their prestige.

Americans have not abandoned their love for very casual clothing. Jeans makers have been weathering a severe drop-off in sales from the heady "Western look" days of the late 1970s,

---

[1] The Paris couture shows are held in January (spring and summer collections) and July (fall and winter). The ready-to-wear shows are held in March (fall and winter) and October (spring and summer).

but blue denim is still ubiquitous. The physical fitness craze has turned exercise clothes, from baggy gray sweatsuits to sleek leotards and satin shorts, into items of fashion. "Who ever thought that wearing a pair of swim trunks or basketball shorts over a pair of felt pants would be a fashion look?" said Norman Karr, executive director of the Men's Fashion Association of America in New York.[2] Faddish trends regarded as extreme, from the "punk" look to the foppish androgyny of rock star Prince, also affect the way Americans dress.

The revitalized American interest in fashion has buoyed an apparel industry that nonetheless is beset with serious disputes and problems. Along with the concern over designer-name over-kill, many department stores and boutiques are angered by the appearance of designer clothes in the burgeoning discount or "off-price" stores. Also worrisome is the tidal wave of imports that threatens to swamp domestic clothing manufacture.

The Fashion Leaders of Europe and Asia

To many Americans, the term "Paris original" still epitomizes the height of fashion. It was Paris that gave the world haute couture (literally, "high sewing"). The famous names of Paris fashion, such as Yves St. Laurent, the House of Dior and the House of Chanel, are familiar even to Americans who cannot afford their creations. Paris fashion shows still outdraw those held in other cities.

High fashion operates on two levels. The heart of couture is the made-to-order business, enjoyed by a relative handful of the world's wealthiest people. Famous couturiers personally design their fashions to meet the whims and shapes of their upper-crust clients. The honor of owning a one-of-a-kind designer original is dearly bought though; prices of $5,000 for a dress and over $50,000 for formal evening attire are not unusual.

Diminishing clienteles and the high cost of labor and materials nearly doomed haute couture a decade ago, but the fashion houses are making a comeback. Money from the nouveau riche of the Middle East, South America and Asia helped; and in the last few years, the strength of the U.S. dollar, which can now purchase more relative to foreign currencies, has increased the interest of America's wealthy in European haute couture. "Today, the couture is as strong as it has ever been, with the twice-yearly Paris showings attracting an ever-growing number of customers who apparently can well afford the steep tariffs," *New York Times* fashion writer Carrie Donovan wrote recently. The strong dollar "has brought more customers from the United

---

[2] Karr and others quoted in this report were interviewed by the author unless otherwise noted.

States than have been seen in the salons since the 1930s," she added.[3]

Even in these flush times, few couturiers prosper from their made-to-order designs alone. Most have ready-to-wear lines. It is to the ready-to-wear or "prêt-à-porter" shows near Versailles to which hundreds of buyers, including those from upscale American department stores such as Bloomingdale's, Saks Fifth Avenue, Neiman Marcus and I. Magnin, flock to purchase the seasonal lines. "This semiannual circus of thin models, expensive clothes, wild parties and high-voltage egos isn't merely another media event," Marcia Berss wrote in *Forbes* magazine. "In one week a department store team may buy clothes that tally 10 percent of its annual apparel sales."[4] Although not nearly as expensive as the personally crafted haute couture, these ready-to-wear items are not found in the bargain basement; *Forbes* showed how a designer wool coat, purchased wholesale for $407, would retail for $1,345 after the markup, overhead, taxes and customs duties are added in.

Unlike the old days in Paris, no single couturier today is powerful enough to act as arbiter for the fashion world. The American woman who still looks to Paris for guidance must consider several distinct and often contrasting fashion messages: the elegance of Saint Laurent and Karl Lagerfeld, for example, or the more idiosyncratic tastes of Claude Montana and Sonia Rykiel. "Even with the most cursory previews of the Paris ready-to-wear collections, there are usually hints of common fashion themes," fashion writer Patricia McColl reported last October. "But ... as the designers prepare to show their clothes for next spring and summer ... the message seems to be: To each his own."[5]

Paris itself has lost its single-handed domination of the world of fashion. Giorgio Armani and Gianni Versace are two of the popular designers based in Milan, which has supplanted Florence and Rome as Italy's fashion center. London, a hot spot in the 1960s during the days of the Mod look and the miniskirt, is on the rise again, with the classical look of Jean Muir, the romantic styling of Laura Ashley, the flamboyance of Zandra Rhodes, and the offbeat, punk- and New Wave-inspired fashions of Katherine Hamnett, the Body Map group and others. The baggy and unconstructed look created by Japanese designers — Issey Miyake, Rei Kawakubo and Yohji Yamamoto among them — burst upon the fashion world in 1982 and 1983.

---

[3] Carrie Donovan, "The Paris Couture: A Combination of Conspicuous Consumption and Elegant Experimentation," *The New York Times Magazine*, Sept. 16, 1984, p. 113.

[4] Marcia Berss, "Paris, When It Sizzles," *Forbes*, April 23, 1984, pp. 48-51.

[5] Patricia McColl, "Paris Goes Its Own Way," *The New York Times Magazine*, Oct. 14, 1984, pp. 101-108.

This competition has spurred the governments of several countries to promote their fashion industries, which serve both as profitable exporters and as symbols of national creativity. Last year, British Prime Minister Margaret Thatcher held a reception at her official residence for members of the fashion industry; a similar event was held in Paris' Elysée Palace. Several French commentators have noted with some irony that haute couture, a symbol of capitalistic consumption, has received more direct assistance from the Socialist government of François Mitterrand than from the more conservative administrations that preceded it.

Middle Class Target for U.S. Designers

The United States has emerged as an important center of fashion creativity in its own right. A number of American couturiers are recognized as among the world's best. These include James Galanos, who was presented with a "lifetime achievement" award by the Council of Fashion Designers of America at a dinner in New York Jan. 13. Although not a household name like many other top designers, Galanos has been in the business since 1952 and has built a reputation for quality that has won him the loyalty of many wealthy and famous women, including first lady Nancy Reagan. "The audience for a Galanos design is a limited one," Carrie Donovan wrote. "It consists of women who very obviously have a considerable amount of cash to spend on clothes, women who are appreciative of original design but are even more concerned about quality of workmanship and longevity of wearability." [6]

Galanos is unusual among American designers in a couple of ways. He works in Los Angeles; most are based in New York City, mainly in the Garment District along Seventh Avenue, which has been nicknamed "Fashion Avenue." Galanos is also one of the few American designers who intentionally restrict their clientele; Galanos markets his ready-to-wear designs in less than 30 high-fashion stores and boutiques across the country. Most other designers, even those who have exclusive couture lines as well, market their ready-to-wear clothes much more pervasively than Galanos does.

In fact, since the late 1970s, most of America's major designers have been trying to appeal to middle- and upper-middle-class consumers with moderately priced fashion lines.[7] The decision to produce these lines was in part due to the demands of consumers, particularly the millions of working women, for

---

[6] Carrie Donovan, "Galanos: An American Original," *New York Times Magazine*, Oct. 21, 1984, pp. 77-80.
[7] While prices vary considerably, many designers suggest retail prices of $250-$300 and under for their moderately-priced items.

stylish, affordable clothing, and in part because of the need to diversify. "Economic survival requires designers to develop more modern marketing techniques targeted to different market segments," said Frank Mori, president of Anne Klein Inc. "To continue to put all your eggs in one basket is the way to economic demise." [8] Anne Klein's top designers, Donna Karan and Louis Dell'Olio, introduced their "Anne Klein II" line in 1983. [9] Other designers with moderately priced lines include Oscar de la Renta ("Miss O"), Bill Blass ("Bill Blass III"), Geoffrey Beene ("Geoffrey Beene, Part Two") and Halston ("Halston III," for J. C. Penney).

Several mass-apparel manufacturers, such as Palm Beach Inc. of Cincinnati with its Evan-Picone line, have long produced stylish clothing aimed at working women. But the fastest growing company in this field is the one founded by New York designer Liz Claiborne. Started with a grubstake of $250,000 in 1976, Liz Claiborne Inc. earned about $360 million in revenue in 1984, up from $229 million in 1983. "The ranks of the career working women, Claiborne's consumers, are over 12 million strong and growing 10 percent a year," Howard Rudnitsky wrote in *Forbes.* "They spend a big piece of their paycheck on the right kinds of  clothes, and Liz Claiborne has her customer's number." [10]

Most successful ready-to-wear lines are based on the concept of "separates": skirts, blouses, jackets, sweaters, blazers and other items sold individually so that they can be combined to create their own fashion identity. "It is no longer a crime to wear a skirt that is very long, or a skirt that ends above the knee," said Kurt Barnard, publisher of *Barnard's Retail Marketing Report* and former executive director of the Federation of Apparel Manufacturers in New York. "In fact, nobody cares. It is what you want, that is what counts."

Some commentators say that this fashion independence has been somewhat negated by the "dress-for-success" or "executive

---

[8] Quoted in *Advertising Age,* Sept. 5, 1983.
[9] Anne Klein, who founded the fashion company named for her, died in 1974.
[10] Howard Rudnitsky, "What's in a Name?" *Forbes,* March 12, 1984, pp. 43-44.

dressing" movement that began in the mid-1970s. Seeking to overcome stereotypes and prejudices against female employees and prompted by how-to guides like John Molloy's *Dress for Success*, many women who thought they had freed themselves from fashion dictates found themselves dressing to fit in at the office. In April 1983, Walter Kiechel III noted in *Fortune* the dominance of the "two-piece suit with a blouse and a neat little bow tie" among upwardly mobile working women. "The point, of course, is to blend in," Kiechel wrote. "In particular, you should avoid outdoing your superior." [11]

Barnard agreed that many working women have adopted a very conservative style of business dress. The career-minded woman "may actually want to look severe," he said. "She probably wants to blend into a business environment, and not be singled out as, 'Ah, she's a woman executive.' " But Barnard added that "women are once again becoming more feminine in the way they dress outside the office," noting that the dress, out of vogue since pants and separates gained dominance in the 1970s, is making a comeback. Femininity is also making its way into executive dressing. According to Tina Sutton, fashion editor for *Savvy* magazine, "Women are no longer feeling obligated to wear navy blue suits and white blouses. Most working women today want a softer look." [12]

Menswear: Return to the Suit and Tie

If the fashion world is centered on what women wear, it is because most American men traditionally have shown little interest in fashion. Nonetheless, many of the top designers have profitable menswear lines — Bill Blass, Oscar de la Renta, Ralph Lauren, Yves St. Laurent and Pierre Cardin among them. "Most men in this country and most other countries do not want to be considered as fashion-conscious," Norman Karr of the Men's Fashion Association said. "They do want to be considered as image-aware." For over a decade, the image for many men, especially young adults, was individualistic and anti-establishment. But as men were caught up in the "executive dressing" trend — Molloy's original *Dress for Success* book was aimed at men — the predominant image became that of the Organization Man.

While the gray-flannel suit may not be the uniform that it was in the 1950s — navy blue and other dark shades are popular today — it is clear that dressing up is back. "More than ever, it seems that men have a firm grasp on what it means 'to dress,' " fashion reporter John Duka wrote. "For them, that simply means dressing in a manner that is traditional or, as one reads

[11] Walter Kiechel III, "The Managerial Dress Code," *Fortune*, April 4, 1983, pp. 193-196.
[12] Quoted in *USA Today*, Jan. 15, 1985.

incessantly, classical, rather than buying clothes with tricky shapes, outlandish colors, numerous details and styling that is too redolent of the past." [13]

There is a Golden Rule of business dressing, Karr said: "He who has the gold, makes the rules." He explained, "All of the junior executives and the junior-junior executives copy the boss, because that's what you do, that's the game. If he's wearing a yellow tie, then yellow ties are in." This adult game of follow-the-leader does not surprise Karr. "Most people are bound to be conservative," he said. "Most people don't like to be laughed at, they don't like to be teased, they don't like to be on the grill. . . . The man who wants to be the first on his block with something new, he is generally the rarity."

Last year the Men's Fashion Association revived the "Look of Success" booklet it published in the late 1950s and early 1960s. Karr said that the tips given in the booklet have not changed significantly over the past 25 years, except that "the tone of it isn't as strident. . . . The idea years ago was that you had to impose these things on people." Dress codes are no longer mandated, but "suggested," he said. Although the business suit uniform has again become a stereotype, Karr said that "a lot more people are wearing sports coats and slacks to work than they ever did before."

Casual Style of Athletic, Leisure Clothes

The youths of the 1960s who adopted blue jeans as standard apparel were rebelling against the established rules of society. In doing so, however, they grandly benefited a number of established corporate interests, namely blue-jean manufacturers like Levi Strauss, Lee and Wrangler. By the end of the 1970s, jeans had been adopted as the national casual uniform even by many starchy suburban matrons and by men who had formerly attended baseball  games in white shirt and tie. Jean sales boomed even further in the late 1970s and early 1980s, spurred by the "Western look" creations of designer Ralph Lauren, the popularity of the movie "Urban Cowboy," and the faddish craze for jeans with a designer name sewn on the back pocket.

Karr does not believe that the turn toward fashion conser-

---

[13] John Duka, "Fashions and Men's Lives," *The New York Times Magazine* (special men's fashion section), March 25, 1984, pp. 90-91.

vatism has seriously affected Americans' love for denim. "The jeans generation still jumps into its jeans on weekends," he said. "The idea that jeans are dead is nonsense." But if people are still seen in jeans, a lot of them must be wearing old pairs; the sales of the major jeans makers are down. In 1984, Levi Strauss' sales fell 8 percent from the year before, and the company's profit dropped 79 percent. Levi Strauss and several other manufacturers are giving new emphasis to their other product lines, such as shirts, dress slacks, corduroys and colored jeans.

The jeans slump hardly means a return to prim propriety in casual wear. The current interest in fitness has sparked a desire to show off the body, or at least to show it off in clothes identified with exercise. Women are seen on the street in loose-fitting runner's T-shirts or in shorts over form-fitting leotards, looks that offset the conservatism of much of today's sportswear and office apparel. Muscle shirts and short shorts are in for men, too. Stylish, colorful jogging suits are de rigueur for the supermarket as well as the gymnasium.

Also popular is the outdoors look, even among those for whom the great outdoors is Central Park or the backyard barbecue. Outdoors clothing retailers like L. L. Bean, Eddie Bauer, Cabera's and the Banana Republic have done a booming business over the last decade in chamois and flannel shirts, hiking boots, safari gear and jackets and vests filled with down or weatherproof synthetics such as Gore-Tex or Thinsulate. "... [T]he outdoors is definitely in," Richard Wolkomir wrote in *Smithsonian* magazine. "Advertising men are hiking through midtown Manhattan in mountaineering gear and gum-soled hunting boots. High school students all over the country are stalking their hallways in hunter's camouflage and plaid shooting jackets." [14]

Fashion independence aside, Americans, especially the media-inundated young, are still vulnerable to fads. According to Karr, "a football player sitting on the sidelines at the Super Bowl wearing a T-shirt that, for reasons nobody can really explain, is cut off halfway down his chest, suddenly becomes the jock look that half the kids in the world want to imitate, even at the risk of going around with colds in their lower chests."

[14] Richard Wolkomir, "High-Tech Materials Blaze Urban Trail for Outdoorsy Duds," *Smithsonian*, January 1985, pp. 122-137.

While athletes are influential, movie and rock stars are the big trend-setters for young Americans. There is not as much uniformity as there was during the 1960s when the Beatles first popularized long hair, then psychedelic colors, then army surplus clothing among millions of young people. Today the blue-collar look of rock singer Bruce Springsteen, the tailored and sophisticated appearance of former glitter-rocker David Bowie, and the peg-panted, epauletted, white-socks-and-black-shoes garb of Michael Jackson exist side-by-side in high school hallways.

Some teenagers have adopted even more extreme styles: the Edwardian flounces and purple suits worn by Prince, the tie-dyed hair and "bag lady look" of Cyndi Lauper, the spiky-coiffed and leather-strapped "punk" look, or the flamboyant androgyny of Boy George O'Dowd of the group Culture Club. As usual, these fads are ephemeral. "They are more short-lived than ever before," Barnard said. "The Michael Jackson fad is already passing. How long did it live? A couple of seasons."

Cycles of Style

A LTHOUGH CLOTHING, jewelry and hair styles have been status symbols throughout history, most researchers date "fashion" back only to the Middle Ages. "It was in the second half of the fourteenth century that clothes both for men and for women took on new forms, and something emerges which we can already call 'fashion,'" wrote James Laver in *Costume and Fashion: A Concise History* (1983).

With the dawning of the Renaissance, clothing fashions took on an erotic flavor. Men wore colorful clothing and codpieces over their private parts; women's wear featured décolletage (low necklines) and tight corsets. Fashion was originally reserved for royalty, who alone could afford such conspicuous consumption. But with the rise of the middle class, fashion permeated down through society. With no fashion magazines or other mass media, fashion news spread slowly, by use of dolls dressed in replicas of the latest styles or engravings known as "fashion plates." As commoners attempted to dress like kings, royal fashions in several countries became more extreme. Bouffant hairdos, powdered wigs and hoop skirts with piles of crinoline were in vogue until the French Revolution (1789-99) tempered the fashion tastes of the upper crust.

111

Men's clothing began to lose its flamboyance in the early 1800s. George (Beau) Brummell, an English fashion arbiter and friend of royalty, urged men to give up their wigs, elaborate clothes and heavy colognes, which he viewed as cover-ups for poor personal hygiene. Brummell called for a clean, uncomplicated look, with dark colors and straight, tailored lines. One of his innovations was the substitution of trousers for knee-length breeches. While the "dandies" of Brummell's age livened up their conservative outfits with fancy cravats and top hats, they nonetheless set a lasting trend in men's clothing. Well into the 20th century, men's fashions would consist of variations on the basic themes of suits, topcoats and hats.

While men's clothing was divested of sex appeal, women continued to dress in fashions that reflected the concept, named much later, of the "shifting erogenous zones." Clothing would emphasize one part of a woman's body, such as the bosom, until society appeared bored with its exposure and turned its attention to the legs or the waist. Even during the supposedly puritanical Victorian era, décolletage emphasized by corsets was the predominant fashion style. It was during the latter half of the 19th century that couturiers rose to prominence. Charles Frederick Worth, an Englishman who founded the House of Worth in Paris in 1858, was regarded as the first "dictator of fashion."

Though no longer restricted to royalty, fashionable dressing was still available only to the affluent who could afford to hire couturiers or seamstresses to stitch clothing together by hand. The industrial revolution helped make fashion available to the masses. The clothing pattern and the sewing machine were invented in the 1800s; by the turn of the century, American factories filled with immigrant laborers were producing millions of ready-to-wear garments that translated the ideas of French couturiers into affordable imitations for U.S. women.

American Fashion in the 20th Century

The early 20th century was a period of fashion excess: The dominant look for women was the "S-curve," a corseted style that thrust the chest out in one direction and the buttocks out in the other. The years around World War I ushered in a new fashion era. Women shed their corsets and hoops for a simpler, more natural shape. The bustline was de-emphasized as fashionable women pursued an almost boyish appearance; legs were freely displayed for the first time. Gabrielle (Coco) Chanel introduced the "little black dress" that became her fashion trademark throughout her career.

Chanel also popularized items previously seen only in men's wardrobes: trousers, pea jackets, trenchcoats and turtleneck sweaters. The images created by movie stars such as Joan Crawford and Greta Garbo, with their padded-shouldered suits, helped legitimize man-tailoring for women. But women's fashions of the 1930s and 1940s for the most part emphasized "femininity," as the couturiers of the day defined it. Hats, gloves, stockings and high-heeled shoes were fashion necessities. If fashion dictated a prominent bust, then American women cantilevered themselves into "push-up" brassieres. When Christian Dior's "New Look," introduced in the late 1940s, brought back the "wasp" waist, women poured themselves into girdles nearly as constricting as the old-fashioned corsets.

"Beau" Brummell

This passion for fashion, reinforced by postwar affluence, a thriving domestic apparel manufacturing industry, the fashion press, and the nascent American couture houses, carried into the 1950s. "We waited each year for the announcement from Paris regarding next year's hemline," said Ellen Melinkoff, author of *What We Wore: An Offbeat Social History of Women's Clothing, 1950 to 1980* (1984). "Newspapers and magazines played along, giving front-page coverage to the long-anticipated, dreaded measurement . . . Paris would tell us what was fashionable. When the word finally leaked out, the top couturiers specifying an inch shorter or three inches longer, it was given the authority of a papal bull. We meekly made adjustments to our skirts so we wouldn't look provincial."

Melinkoff noted that comfort and practicality were often sacrificed in the name of fashion. Describing the "New Look," she wrote: "To pull off this look successfully required a considerable amount of infrastructure, the Sherman tank line of corsetry. The natural female figure was merely raw material that had to be poured, molded, whittled to perfection. How did it feel to be living sculpture? Awful. But we endured in the name of womanhood."

American fashion in the early 1960s was dominated by a figure of traditional feminine elegance and haute couture, Jacqueline Kennedy. Many women imitated her style of simple suits and pillbox hats. But a fashion revolution was already under way, first in England and France, then in America. Mary

Quant in London and André Courrèges in Paris pioneered the miniskirt; soon hemlines rose to unprecedented heights. The widespread marketing of pantyhose enabled women to shed their girdles while maintaining a semblance of modesty. The shiftlike outfits de-emphasized the bust, freeing women from distorting bra styles. Bathing suits grew skimpier, as society's version of propriety liberalized. The late 1960s saw growing acceptance of another fashion style: pantsuits for women. Even men started to shake their gray-flannel image, adopting elements of the London "Mod" look with its bold colors, Nehru jackets and paisley prints. Some fashion observers predicted that men would be swept away by a "Peacock Revolution."

Designers' Hold Loosened by Midi's Flop

After several years of the miniskirt, French designers in 1970 tried to reassert their control over the American woman's fashion psyche by promoting the midi-skirt. Women overwhelmingly said no. The drastic drop in hemlines from thigh to mid-calf was seen as a conspiracy by designers to force women to buy entirely new wardrobes. A group of socialites founded an organization called POOFF (Preservation of Our Femininity and Finances) to protest the midi. Members of the women's liberation movement viewed the midi as an attempt to return women to unwieldy and impractical clothing styles.

At the same time that the midi flopped, the war in Vietnam and the civil rights movement were radicalizing many young Americans who came to see fashion as a symbol of a wasteful, affluent establishment. Those swept up in the youth movement took to "dressing down." Faded blue jeans, tie-dyed T-shirts, peasant dresses, surplus army fatigues, sandals and hiking boots became the anti-fashion fashion, almost to the point of bringing conformity to the non-conformists.

The 1970s became a "do your own thing" decade as far as fashion was concerned. The country was still swept by fads, but many of them came out of the streets and film studios rather than the couturier salons. Hot pants and platform shoes enjoyed brief bursts of popularity. A few people still have a disco outfit or two, bought after seeing the 1977 movie *Saturday Night Fever*, hanging in the backs of their closets. Other movies sparked fashion trends: "Annie Hall" gave women oversized men's clothes and floppy hats, "Urban Cowboy" spurred the Western look. The preppy look, a style earlier known as "collegiate" or "Ivy League" and identified with wealthy white-Anglo-Saxon Protestants, perhaps presaged the growing conservatism in American dress and politics. Women dressed in plaid skirts and blazers, men in shetland sweaters and crisp flannel slacks, and everyone in Izod "alligator" shirts and topsider shoes.

Market Worries

I N THE FASHION WORLD, the 1970s ended as they began: it was the decade of denim. "Women in the seventies could wear anything, but all they wanted to wear was jeans," Melinkoff wrote. "With the riches of the world available to them, they dressed with the monotonous uniformity of medieval serfs." But the jeans being worn as the 1980s dawned were only cousins to those of 10 years earlier. Then, denims were faded, baggy, patched, decorated with peace-sign appliques. The jeans of 1980 were tight, tailored, pressed and embellished only with the distinctive stitching and the label of a high-fashion designer.

The designer jeans craze was the most widespread fashion trend of the past decade. Worn skintight, a style adopted from the disco scene, these pants were treated more like couture than casual wear. "We dry-cleaned our jeans, babying them like the most delicate silks," Melinkoff wrote. The jeans boom, heavily promoted through advertising, filled the coffers of a number of well-known designers — including Calvin Klein, Gloria Vanderbilt and Pierre Cardin — and several Johnny-come-lately apparel manufacturers, like Jordache and Sasson.

Americans may have been unwilling to kowtow to dictatorial designers, but they were not averse to wearing designer labels or initials on the outside of their clothing for all the world to see. Pants, jackets, shirts, belts, ties and other articles of clothing were emblazoned with famous names or trademarks. Tote bags with "Gucci" or Yves St. Laurent's "YSL" signature printed on them were especially sought after. The sudden mass popularity of designer insignias was like a gold rush for well-known designers, who licensed the use of their names to manufacturers of numerous ready-to-wear clothing items and accessories, including colognes, footwear, luggage, handbags, umbrellas, even home decorating items like furniture and shower curtains. Bill Blass lent his name to a line of expensive chocolates, and the R. J. Reynolds Tobacco Co. is test-marketing a line of cigarettes designed by Yves St. Laurent in Atlanta, Memphis, Oklahoma City and the state of Washington.

This widespread marketing of designers' names concerns many in the fashion industry. They fear that high-fashion design may lose its cachet, its exclusiveness, if designers' names are spread wide-and-thin on mundane items over which the designers themselves have little creative input. Because an item is no longer a status symbol if it is owned by millions of people, critics say that extensive licensing threatens to reduce couteriers to the level of less ritzy manufacturers in the public eye. The designers, however, defend the practice, saying that it provides profits which support their less efficient and more risky haute couture lines.

Wide Distribution, Discounting Deplored

The friendly relationship between designers and exclusive department stores may be turning sour, for reasons similar to the licensing controversy. The prestigious stores formerly "adopted" designers, providing them with their own sections in the stores. In return, designers agreed to sell their clothes only in that store or, at most, one or two others in the same market area. In recent years, however, designers seeking higher sales and better economies-of-scale began to offer their lines to several stores in an area.

Department store owners complained about over-saturation of designer goods. "At least a half a dozen stores carried them, so there was absolutely no advantage to [a customer] to go to any one store in preference to another," Kurt Barnard said. "The image of the store became submerged and it was the image of the label, of the designer, that really dominated the customers' thinking." With the distinctiveness of their clothing lines diminished, the stores turned to the chancy tactic of price competition to draw customers. "[If] you find an ad by Store X showing a Calvin Klein garment at $59.95, while facing it is the ad by the competition with a price of $49.95, where are you going to buy that garment?" Barnard asked.

Department stores were particularly piqued when designers whose names they touted for their "snob appeal" started designing for mass-merchandise chains, as Halston did by contracting with J. C. Penney.[15] Designer clothes also began to turn up in "off-price" clothing stores, one of the fastest growing segments of the retail industry. These chains — Loehmann's, Marshall's, T. J. Maxx, Hit or Miss and Syms are among the best known — buy manufacturers' overruns, orders canceled by department stores, irregulars and "end-of-season" runs, direct from manufacturers or through middlemen, for fire-sale prices. These discounts, combined with the low overhead of their no-frills, "piperack" operations, enable the off-pricers to sell items, including those with a designer label, for a fraction of what they cost at nearby department stores *(see chart, p. 118)*.

Several department stores have retaliated by dropping the

---

[15] In August 1984, Kenzo Takada, the Paris-based Japanese designer, followed suit by signing a contract to design clothes for The Limited Stores, a 550-unit chain specializing in inexpensive clothing. Shortly after the agreement was announced, the R. H. Macy department store in New York said it was dropping Kenzo's couture collection.

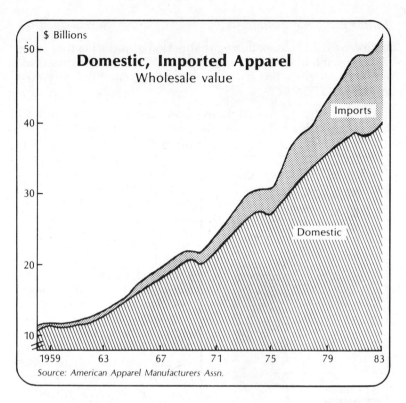

Domestic, Imported Apparel
Wholesale value

$ Billions

Imports

Domestic

1959   63   67   71   75   79   83

Source: American Apparel Manufacturers Assn.

lines of designers whose goods turn up in discount or off-price stores. Among them is Sakowitz, the Houston-based department store chain, which in the last few years has extensively marketed its own "private label" clothing. According to Barnard, private label products, the mainstays of department store merchandise a half-century ago, are being emphasized as stores attempt to "recapture the identity which they lost many years ago when they began to adopt designers." Singling out the Dayton Co. of Minneapolis for its success with its "Boundary Waters" line, Barnard said private labels may enable department stores to re-establish themselves as important market forces, but added that they will never regain the status they once had. "There are now too many other forms of retailing around," he said. "The off-pricer is here to stay, the discount department store is here to stay...."

U.S. Apparel Industry's Import Problems

Department stores are not the only entities troubled by recent trends in the apparel industry; so are domestic manufacturers. The problem is not that Americans are not spending money on clothing. Expenditures for apparel and accessories went up from $22.2 billion in 1960 to nearly $100 billion in 1982. Even measuring in 1972 dollars to account for inflation, consumer apparel expenditures more than doubled, from $30.1

billion to $72.1 billion, during that period. But during that same 20-year stretch, clothing imports to the United States boomed, creating a serious threat to the domestic apparel industry *(see chart, p. 117).*

In 1964, imports of cotton, wool and man-made fiber apparel amounted to 561 million square yards. By 1974, that figure had more than tripled, to 1.94 billion square yards. Between 1974 and 1983, the square yardage doubled to 3.87 billion. As a percentage of all U.S. retail apparel sales, imports increased from 12 percent in 1975 to 25 percent in 1983. In that year, imports accounted for $24 billion of the $97 billion retail apparel market. The import surge is not only in inexpensive, mass-merchandised clothing lines. Although most of the top designers maintain quality control over their top-of-the-line designs by having them cut in their own workshops, many of them farm out their more modestly priced garments for overseas manufacture.

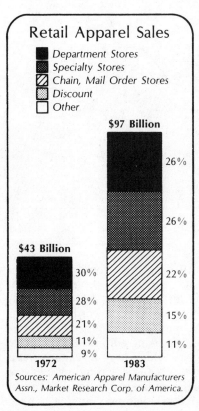

Retail Apparel Sales

- ■ Department Stores
- ▨ Specialty Stores
- ▧ Chain, Mail Order Stores
- ▦ Discount
- ☐ Other

$97 Billion
26%
26%
22%
15%
11%

$43 Billion
30%
28%
21%
11%
9%

1972   1983

Sources: American Apparel Manufacturers Assn., Market Research Corp. of America.

The main reason for the import tide is the availability of cheap labor in Third World nations. The apparel industry in the United States is still a major employer of recent immigrants, who are hardly getting rich off their labor: The average hourly wage in 1982, according to the U.S. Department of Labor, was $5.20, well below that in most other heavily unionized industries. But the wage rate is princely compared with those of other countries. The hourly wage was $1.80 in Hong Kong, $1.50 in Taiwan, $1.00 in South Korea and 20 cents in the People's Republic of China.

Those nations are the "Big Four" in U.S. apparel imports, accounting for 69 percent of the total in 1983. Taiwan was the leader (859 million square yards), followed by Hong Kong (758 million) and South Korea (635 million). China, which did not even have trade relations with the United States until 1972, exported 430 million square yards to this country in 1983. The Philippines and India have enjoyed rapidly rising shares of the U.S. apparel market, though Japan, whose own wage rates have been on the rise, has seen its exports to the U.S. decline. Other countries that exported more than 50 million square yards of apparel to the U.S. in 1983 were Singapore, the Dominican Republic, Sri Lanka, Thailand, Haiti, Mexico and Macao. The European countries of haute couture have relatively little impact on the U.S. apparel trade.

Imports have had a severe impact on employment in the domestic apparel industry. In 1973, 1,438,000 people, mostly women, were employed in the American apparel industry. By 1982, employment had declined by 19 percent, to 1,163,700. In some states, the decline has been sharper. In New York, the historic center of the garment industry, employment fell from 235,300 to 157,100 (33 percent) in that period. In Illinois, garment industry employment fell by 43 percent.

The import surge has taken place despite the existence of an intricate code of protective legislation, described in 1983 by economist William Niskanen Jr. as a "Byzantine web of country-by-country, product-by-product quotas." [16] The textile industry is urging the Reagan administration to tighten import quotas when it enters negotiations, expected to start in June, to renew the worldwide system of textile quotas.[17] Despite its general opposition to trade restraints, the administration has decided to go ahead with a rule issued last October to control "transshipments," the practice of making a garment in more than one country but labeling it as made in the country with more room to spare under existing import quotas. Domestic textile makers backed the new rule but retailers said it would disrupt longstanding orders, and Hong Kong manufacturers said the new rule threatened their entire business.

The apparel industry has been affected, like other American industries, by the strong U.S. dollar that benefits imports and penalizes exports. "As the strength of the dollar decreases in the future, the level of demand is likely to diminish somewhat for foreign apparel," said the American Apparel Manufacturers Association in a 1984 report entitled "Apparel Manufacturing Strategies." But, the report warned, "by itself a weaker dollar will not significantly improve the competitive position of domestic apparel in the future. Many LDC's [less-developed countries] will continue to offer apparel at prices below U.S. prices because of much lower labor and other costs and other incentives and subsidies that keep costs from rising."

[16] Quoted in *Forbes*, Aug. 1, 1983.
[17] See Art Pine, "U.S. Textile Industry Launches Effort to Further Restrict Foreign Imports," *The Wall Street Journal*, March 18, 1985.

Selected Bibliography

Books

Fraser, Kennedy, *The Fashionable Mind: Reflections on Fashion, 1970-1981*, Alfred A. Knopf, 1981.

Laver, James, *Costume & Fashion: A Concise History*, Oxford University Press, 1983.

Melinkoff, Ellen, *What We Wore: An Offbeat Social History of Women's Clothing, 1950 to 1980*, William Morrow & Co., 1984.

Molloy, John T., *The Woman's Dress for Success Book*, Follett Publishing Co., 1977.

Articles

Berss, Marcia, "Paris, When It Sizzles," *Forbes*, April 23, 1984.

Borrus, Amy, "The Bold and the Kooky Have British Fashion Strutting Again," *Business Week*, Jan. 28, 1985.

Hollander, Anne, "Dressed to Thrill," *The New Republic*, Jan. 28, 1985.

Kiechel, Walter III, "The Managerial Dress Code," *Fortune*, April 4, 1983.

McCarroll, Thomas, "Beyond the Blues Horizon," *Time*, Aug. 20, 1984.

Morrison, Ann M., "The Upshot of Off-Price," *Fortune*, June 13, 1983.

Salholz, Eloise et al., "Smart Shoppers for Hire," *Newsweek*, June 25, 1984.

Taylor, Alexander L. III et al., "Rough Times in the Rag Trade," *Time*, Aug. 29, 1983.

The New York Times Magazine (Fashion section), various issues.

Wolkomir, Richard, "High-Tech Materials Blaze Urban Trail for Outdoorsy Duds," *Smithsonian*, January 1985.

"Word from Fashion Moguls: Do Your Own Thing," *U.S. News & World Report*, May 9, 1983.

Reports and Studies

American Apparel Manufacturers Association, "Apparel Manufacturing Strategies," 1984.

——, "Apparel Import Digest," 1983 annual issue.

Editorial Research Reports: "Fashion World," 1971 Vol. I, p. 269.

Graphics: Cover by Guy Aceto; pp. 107,109,110,113 and 118 by Assistant Art Director Robert Redding, p. 117 by Staff Artist Kathleen Ossenfort.

THE
BOOK
BUSINESS

by

Marc Leepson

June 28
1 9 8 5

THE BOOK BUSINESS

BOOK PUBLISHING is one of the most visible, influential and varied industries in the United States. It is made up of giant corporations with billion-dollar balance sheets as well as "Mom and Pop" businesses that turn out one or two books a year. More than 50,000 titles, covering nearly every conceivable topic, are published annually. Elementary, high school and college texts gross about $2.5 billion a year for their publishers, while libraries purchase hundreds of millions of dollars' worth of books.

The storehouse of knowledge contained in the more than 600,000 books in print in the United States — as well as in the incalculable number of out-of-print titles — is an essential part of the fabric of society. Books spread ideas and information, stir imaginations and provide entertainment. Yet, as the figures indicate, book publishing is a big business, and the clash between business goals and cultural objectives is a continuing conflict for authors, publishers and booksellers.

The industry is made up of more than 15,000 publishers whose books are divided into five broad categories: (1) trade books, (2) textbooks, (3) technical, scientific and professional books, (4) religious books and (5) reference books.[1] With the exception of reference books, the industry had a good year in 1984. According to the U.S. Department of Commerce, book publishers' sales added up to a record $9.4 billion in 1984, an increase of 5.1 percent over 1983. A record 2.27 billion books were sold at the retail level, bringing in nearly $12.9 billion last year, a 7.2 percent increase over 1983, according to the Center for Book Research.[2] Profits "grew rapidly in 1984, helped by low inventory levels, a tight rein on costs, and reduced rates of inflation," the Commerce Department reported.[3]

[1] The 1983-84 edition of *Books in Print* listed 15,200 publishers; some industry analysts believe there may be as many as 20,000 publishers. In 1983 the number of new titles and new editions published totaled 53,380, indicating that most publishing operations are very small.

[2] The Center for Book Research, an industry-supported non-profit organization, is located at the University of Scranton in Pennsylvania.

[3] U.S. Department of Commerce, "U.S. Industrial Outlook 1985," p. 27—6. The Association of American Publishers (AAP) estimates that book publishers' sales for 1984 were $9.1 billion, a 6.2 percent increase over AAP's estimated 1983 sales *(See table, p. 489)*. The association represents the interests of large publishing houses in all categories of books.

Publishers' sales, however, were sluggish during the fourth quarter of 1984 and in the first three months of 1985. According to data compiled by John Dessauer, director of the Center for Book Research, the number of books sold by publishers declined 4.3 percent in January-March 1985 compared with sales in those three months in 1984. Still, because of price increases, publishers took in 5.8 percent more in sales. The Commerce Department remains optimistic about the industry's financial picture, predicting that U.S. publishers' shipments will increase at an average annual rate of 3.5 percent, adjusted for price changes, from 1985-89. Sales and earnings, the department predicts, should reach "record levels during this period."

Mixed Economic News for Trade Houses

Trade publishers, who put out hardcover and paperback books sold primarily in bookstores and through book clubs, account for about 30 percent of all book sales, some $3 billion in 1984. Hardcover trade books had a particularly notable year. Bantam Books' *Iacocca*, the autobiography of Chrysler Chairman Lee Iacocca, sold more than a million copies in two months to become the fastest-selling hardcover book ever published. Viking's 600,000-copy first printing of the horror novel *The Talisman* by Stephen King and Peter Straub was the largest first printing in the history of hardcover novels. Each of the 15 top-selling novels and an unprecedented 19 non-fiction hardcover books (primarily how-to, business and cookbooks) sold more than 200,000 copies in 1984.[4] "This was the first year that the industry has had even as many as 15 fiction titles that sold over 200,000 hardcover units," said Patrick Filley, vice president and editorial director of Doubleday. "Not too long ago there were only about 25 that sold 100,000."[5]

There are two categories of paperback books. Mass market paperbacks, which were developed in 1939 by Robert Fair de Graff of Pocket Books, are the smaller, rack-sized books sold on newsstands, in drugstores, supermarkets, airports and bus stations, as well as in bookstores. A handful of large publishers — Avon, Bantam, Ballantine, Berkley, Fawcett, Dell, New American Library (NAL), Pocket Books and Warner — dominate the category. Trade paperbacks, which are put out by thousands of large and small publishers, are more expensive, larger-sized books that are usually sold in bookstores. Together paperbacks account for more than 50 percent of all bookstore sales.

Paperback sales increased slightly last year but did not set any records. Sales of adult trade paperbacks increased 3.2 per-

---

[4] Sales figures from *Publishers Weekly*, March 15, 1985, "Year in Review" issue, pp. 32-35.

[5] Filley and others quoted in this report were interviewed by the author unless otherwise indicated.

cent over 1983; juvenile trade paperbacks, and mass market paperbacks, 3.8 percent, according to Association of American Publishers' (AAP) estimates.

Overall paperback sales for the first quarter of 1985 have been lackluster. Mass market sales, moreover, have dropped significantly. In the first three months of 1985, according to Dessauer's estimates, publishers' sales of mass market paperbacks fell 13.8 percent from the same period in 1984. Unit sales dropped from more than 164 million in the first quarter of 1984 to about 133 million this year — an 18.8 percent decrease. Adult trade paperback sales were up by less than 1 percent and juvenile trade paperback sales were off by 1.3 percent. Dessauer attributed 1985's "rather disappointing beginning" primarily to the "lukewarm" U.S. economic picture. If the overall economic situation does not brighten, he said, "the prospects for dramatic improvement [in publishers' sales] later in the year are not bright." [6]

Problems, Prospects In Textbook Field

Despite their high visibility, trade books are not the biggest segment of the book publishing industry. That honor goes to elementary, high school and college texts. Although precise figures are unavailable, publishers sold more than $1 billion worth of college texts last year; elementary and secondary school texts grossed about $1.4 billion.

The college text market differs significantly from the elementary and secondary school text market, which is known in publishing circles as "el-hi," largely because of their respective markets. "In elementary and secondary school publishing you're shaping the book for the widest possible market. In many cases it's a state or number of states," said Joanne D. Daniels, director of CQ Press, a college textbook division of Congressional Quarterly Inc.

Some widely used introductory college texts, such as Paul A. Samuelson's *Economics,* now in its 11th edition (McGraw-Hill) and McConnell's *Understanding Human Behavior: An Introduction to Psychology,* now in its fourth edition (Holt, Rinehart & Winston), sell hundreds of thousands of copies. But, Daniels said, in supplementary texts for junior and senior college classes "you're shaping the book for maybe a maximum audience of 10,000 people. And that's very different from talking about school systems of two or three million kids."

College text publishers say one of their biggest problems is the growth in sales of used textbooks. In a recent 12-month period, used-book sales increased 27 percent, compared with a

[6] Writing in *Publishers Weekly,* June 7, 1985, p. 34.

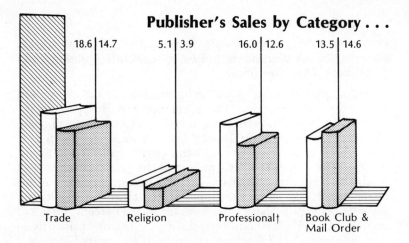

Publisher's Sales by Category . . .

| 18.6 | 14.7 | 5.1 | 3.9 | 16.0 | 12.6 | 13.5 | 14.6 |

Trade   Religion   Professional†   Book Club & Mail Order

† *Includes technical, scientific, business and other professional books.*

Source: Association of American Publishers

17 percent increase in new book sales.[7] Used-book selling "is probably the single most destructive factor that we have to deal with," Daniels said. "The used-book market is extremely aggressive; it is a business of its own. It's a very methodical, a very structural and very successful business." Publishers have tried to discourage used-book sales by shortening the revision cycles of popular texts. "Books used to last four, five, six years," Daniels said. "Now they're lasting one and a half years [before they are revised]."

One thing the two types of textbook publishing have in common is their dependence on enrollments. Colleges experienced such rapid increases in enrollments during the 1960s and 1970s that, as one publishing insider put it, "there was little you could do that didn't make money."[8] By the late 1970s, enrollments leveled off and the college textbook market cooled. But the situation appears to have turned around in the last few years. Increasing college enrollments, the Commerce Department report said, have "pushed annual sales of college textbooks to more than $1 billion, or more than 56 percent of the total U.S. textbook market."[9] The market could constrict again shortly; educators anticipate up to a 15 percent decline in post-secondary education by the mid-1990s. On the elementary school level,

[7] Report covering 1981-82 presented at the 1983 National Association of College Stores Convention. See Thomas W. Gornick, "Higher Education Publishing," in *The Book Publishing Annual* (1984), p. 21.

[8] Thomas Williamson, editor in chief of the college division of Harcourt Brace Jovanovich, quoted in *The Chronicle of Higher Education*, May 23, 1977, p. 7. See also: Lewis A. Coser, *et al.*, *Books: The Culture and Commerce of Publishing* (1982), pp. 55-57.

[9] "U.S. Industrial Outlook," *op. cit.*, p. 27—8. According to the U.S. Department of Education's National Center for Education Statistics, some 12.5 million students were enrolled in the nation's colleges and universities in the fall of 1983, the last year for which complete statistics are available.

... As Percent of Total Sales

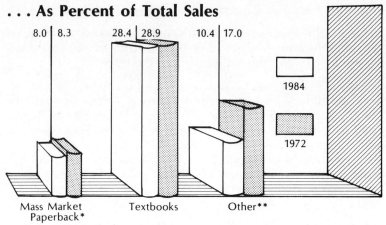

| 8.0 | 8.3 | | 28.4 | 28.9 | | 10.4 | 17.0 |

1984

1972

Mass Market
Paperback* Textbooks Other**

* Rack-size; non-rack-size paperbacks included in trade category.

** Includes university presses, standardized tests, subscription references and audio-visual
and other media materials.

enrollments are projected to begin increasing next year, but high school enrollments will decline until the early 1990s.[10]

At least for the time being, another factor — the growing national demand to improve the quality of education — appears to be working to the advantage of book publishers.[11] "There seems to be a consensus in the United States that education needs to be beefed up, more money be put into it," said William Lofquist, the Commerce Department's publishing industry analyst, "and if you do, you're going to get more textbooks." *The Wall Street Journal* reported that budgetary cutbacks and declining enrollments limited el-hi industry growth to "less than 10% annually in recent years." But the "upsurge in interest in education and a modest increase in elementary-school enrollment," the newspaper said, increased school textbook spending by "13.5 percent for the first 10 months of 1984." [12]

A constant concern of schoolbook publishers is criticism of textbook content. Some parents, teachers and special interest groups have complained about the amount of sex, obscenity and profanity in some books, alleged religious, sexual or racial bias, the undermining of "traditional family values," excessively critical views of U.S. history, the teaching of Darwin's evolutionary theory without reference to the biblical account of creation, and "values clarification" methods of teaching in which students are encouraged to formulate and refine their own

[10] U.S. Department of Education, National Center for Education Statistics, "Conditions of Education," 1985.
[11] For background, see "Status of the Schools," *E.R.R.*, 1984 Vol. II, pp. 609-632.
[12] Bob Davis, "Many Forces Shape Making and Marketing of a New Schoolbook," *The Wall Street Journal*, Jan. 3, 1985.

values.[13] Publishers have made some changes in reaction to outside criticism. Authors have been instructed not to stereotype minority groups and women, for example.

Efforts to challenge — publishers used the word "censor" — text and library books peaked in the early 1980s, especially in the 22 states where a single board approves all the textbooks used in the public schools.[14] "Concern with textbook-selection procedures continues," noted James R. Squire, senior vice president emeritus of Ginn and Co., a school text publisher, "but the alarming increase in complaints about books noted three or four years ago no longer seems characteristic of American education." [15]

Educators have criticized the quality of the writing in school texts and the level of intellectual challenge demanded of students. Former Reagan administration education secretary, Terrel H. Bell, made headlines early in 1984 when he accused school text publishers of "dumbing down" books in order to match what they perceived as lowest common denominator reading levels, thereby reaching a wider audience and heightening sales. Publishers, for their part, say they are ready to provide textbooks at whatever level educators wish. Some publishers even regard the criticism as an incentive to produce and sell more books. "I think that secretly publishers love the publicity," one industry observer commented. "Their response [to criticism] is, 'If you don't like that, take a look at our new set. I think this will meet all of your objections.' "

Sales Picture for Other Book Categories

Technical, scientific and professional or "sci-tech" books — which some analysts believe are the most profitable segment of the industry — accounted for 16 percent of all publishers' sales in 1984. This category includes law books, volumes dealing with the various disciplines of science and technology (including medical books) and all aspects of business, including computers. Very few of these books are sold in all-purpose bookstores. Sci-tech books are more commonly sold by direct mail or in small, specialized bookstores. Many are sold to libraries; some wind up in college classrooms. Prices of sci-tech books are high. According to figures compiled by *Publishers Weekly*, the average price of a hardcover medical book last year was more than $40; the average hardcover science and technology book was more than

---

[13] See "Schoolbook Controversies," *E.R.R.*, 1982 Vol. II, p. 673.
[14] The states are Alabama, Arkansas, California, Florida, Georgia, Hawaii, Indiana, Kentucky, Louisiana, Mississippi, Nevada, New Mexico, North Carolina, Oklahoma, Oregon, South Carolina, Tennessee, Texas, Utah, Virginia, Washington and West Virginia. Procedures vary widely from state to state.
[15] Writing in *The Book Publishing Annual, op. cit.*, p. 25.

$46. In contrast, the average hardcover fiction book cost less than $15.[16] Because of the high prices of hardcover books, many sci-tech publishers have begun issuing books in high-quality softcover editions.

Computer and business books had been the strongest segments of the sci-tech industry in the early 1980s. Last year, however, saw a falloff in computer book sales. The "market for books on personal computers and their programs had become, with nearly 4,000 titles in print, notably overcrowded," *Publishers Weekly* Editor in Chief John F. Baker, commented.[17] Soft sales in computer books forced several publishers to cut their budgets and lay off employees. One computer book publishing company, dilithium Press, filed for bankruptcy in February 1985. The company subsequently cut its staff drastically and is considering acquisition offers from larger publishers.

Business books, on the other hand, continued to sell well in 1984. And because English has become the international language for science and technology, sci-tech publishers have been successful in overseas markets. "A lot of technical book publishers have very large markets overseas," Lofquist said. Other publishers typically export 5-10 percent of their products, he said, but "for technical books it could be anywhere from 20-40 percent."

Sales by religious book houses totaled $461.7 million in 1984, accounting for about 5 percent of industry sales, according to AAP figures. Although overall sales grew by 1.5 percent in 1984, Thomas Nelson, one of the leading religious book publishers, reported that its sales grew by 30 percent for the fifth consecutive year. One Nelson book, *Tough Times Never Last, But Tough People Do!*, by California radio evangelist Robert H. Schuller, was No. 13 on the list of non-fiction hardcover bestsellers in 1984, with more than 226,000 sold. Heightened interest in religion, especially the various fundamentalist Christian branches, accounts for most of the growth. "In the last decade the number of churchgoers has grown by one third," Lofquist said. "A lot of people in fundamentalist sects are big book buyers."

The final main segment of the book publishing industry, reference books, appears to be having the most economic difficulties. Reference books, which include encyclopedias, atlases, dictionaries and directories, are facing hard times because their main client, libraries, have sustained funding cutbacks in the last 10-15 years. "Libraries have had funding problems for a

[16] See table on average per-volume prices of hardcover books, *Publishers Weekly,* March 15, 1985, p. 54.
[17] John F. Baker, "The Year in Publishing," *Publishers Weekly,* March 15, 1985, p. 29.

long time, particularly since around 1972," said Shirley Mills-Fischer, executive director of the Public Library Association. "There's been a constant eroding trend." The funding crunch has led some reference book publishers to experiment with on-line computer operations. Reference book publishers "are sort of covering their bets by publishing a reference book and at the same time making it available through a data base," Lofquist said. "They're protecting themselves for [the time when] instead of buying reference book books, libraries will buy reference data."

Mergers and Acquisitions

THE BIGGEST ISSUE in trade publishing — and to a lesser but significant degree in textbook and reference book publishing as well — is the acquisition of many large and small publishers by large corporations and the merging of smaller publishing firms into larger ones. The result of this rash of mergers and acquisitions is that 12 publishing firms, all parts of multifaceted corporations, took in about 45 percent of the $9.4 billion in book sales in 1983. "The structure of the industry is changing," Townsend Hoopes, president of the Association of American Publishers, said. "There is a shakedown here to a smaller number of larger companies."

Mergers are nothing new in the book publishing business. Over the years many small houses have joined together and weaker publishers have sold out to economically stronger ones. Beginning in the late 1950s the pace of mergers and takeovers began to pick up and in the 1960s and 1970s large corporations such as RCA, CBS, Xerox, ITT, IBM and Time Inc. began buying book publishers.[18] Time, which already owned Time-Life Books, purchased Little, Brown in 1968 and since then has added the Book-of-the-Month Club, the New York Graphic Society and several other smaller book clubs and imprints. CBS numbers Holt, Rinehart and Winston, Praeger Publishers and paperback houses Crest, Popular Library and Gold Medal among its acquisitions. Newhouse Publications, the large newspaper chain, purchased Random House in 1980.

Within the last year there have been two major mergers.[19] The first involved two of the oldest and most profitable American publishing houses, Macmillan Inc. and Scribner Book

[18] See "Book Publishing," *E.R.R.*, 1975 Vol. I, pp. 327-346.
[19] Other publishing mergers in 1984 included Random House's acquisition of Times Books from *The New York Times* and New American Library's purchase of E. P. Dutton.

Companies. In June 1984 the two companies merged, with Scribner agreeing to operate as a Macmillan subsidiary. Founded in 1869, Macmillan publishes about 1,000 books annually. It has separate trade, school, college and medical divisions. Scribner includes three imprints: Charles Scribner's Sons, Atheneum and Rawson Associates. Macmillan last year also acquired Four Winds, a children's imprint, from Scholastic, as well as Harper & Row's schoolbook publishing division. In March 1985 Macmillan purchased ITT's eight publishing companies, including Bobbs-Merrill, G. K. Hall and Howard W. Sams, a technical publisher.

In November 1984 Gulf & Western, the entertainment conglomerate, bought two publishing houses: Esquire Inc., an elementary and high school textbook publisher; and Prentice-Hall, which is the No. 1 college textbook publisher and ranks among the top 10 el-hi publishers. It has some 13,000 titles in print.

Gulf & Western merged its two acquisitions with Simon & Schuster, which it had acquired 10 years before. One of the most successful trade publishers, Simon & Schuster had 19 hardcover best-sellers in 1983-84. A good portion of its list are what *The Wall Street Journal* called "low-brow, high-profit books." These include pulp fiction such as Jackie Collins' *Hollywood Wives* and celebrity exercise books like Victoria Principal's *The Body Principal.* Under the direction of its president, Richard E. Snyder, and editor in chief, Michael Korda, S&S emphasizes promotion, marketing and the bottom line. After the acquisition of Esquire, S&S had $344 million in sales in the 12-month period ending July 31, 1984, with pretax profits of $37 million.[20] The S&S/Prentice-Hall/Esquire merger makes Gulf & Western, which also owns Pocket Books, the nation's largest publisher.

G&W may continue to grow; it has announced its intention to purchase Ginn & Co., one of the leading schoolbook publishers. Ginn is one of six publishing ventures that Xerox Corp., has decided to sell because, according to Xerox President David T. Kearns, their financing needs would have diverted "resources from our mainstream businesses." [21] One of the other publishers Xerox is shedding is R. R. Bowker, a reference book publisher that also owns *Publishers Weekly,* the bible of the publishing industry. Bowker has been bought by International Thompson, a British conglomerate involved in book and magazine publishing, information, and oil and gas ventures. In May Thompson

---

[20] Simon & Schuster financial statistics cited in *The Wall Street Journal,* Sept. 26, 1984.
[21] Quoted in *Publishers Weekly,* May 3, 1985, p.18.

purchased Gale Research Co., a Detroit-based reference book publisher which had sales of more than $30 million in 1984.

Impact of 'Bottom-Line' Considerations

For years the book publishing community has been concerned about the impact of corporate ownership not only on the books that are published but on how the publishing companies are managed. Doubleday's Patrick Filley, for example, spoke of the "MBAism" of corporate-run publishing houses, in which business school trained executives have "brought in words like 'product,' which everybody, especially on the editorial side, gets nervous about using." *Business Week* magazine recently warned that a "common blunder" in corporate mergers, "is an assumption by executives that the skills honed in one business can be readily applied to another." [22]

Some "corporate parents," John Dessauer said, "don't understand the publishing business. So you get situations where there isn't very much enlightenment about what is good publishing. You get some rather narrowly focused, bottom-line oriented perspectives." Harold Roth, a former president of Grosset & Dunlap and now a publishing consultant, agreed. Book publishing, he said, "is like any other art-form business. Anyone who looks simply at the bottom line is going to be in trouble. . . . This is not like banks or steel. [Books are] an artistic, reactive commodity." Concentration on "short-term, bottom-line results" can lead to trouble in publishing, he said, "which, like any other thing that relates to public tastes, has its ups and downs."

Critics claim that the bottom-line pressure has caused publishers to search for and publish the books likely to make a profit and to ignore those of high artistic merit — especially first novels — likely to bring in little or no money. Alfred A. Knopf, who headed the respected literary publishing house that bears his name from 1915 until his death in August 1984, was a vehement critic of the way corporate-owned publishers operated. "In my time, if we had a book we wanted to put out and we knew we couldn't make a profit on it, we would still go ahead and print a relatively small number. My attitude was that this was part of our overhead, and we wrote off the loss before we began," Knopf said in a 1983 interview. "Now, in a world in which many publishers are owned by big conglomerates, it . . . is almost unheard of for them to say, 'It's not going to sell, but we've got to publish it just the same.' "[23]

Most publishers concede that the large corporations generally

[22] Steven E. Prokesch and Teresa Carson, "Do Mergers Really Work?" *Business Week*, June 3, 1985, p. 89.
[23] Quoted in *U.S. News & World Report*, Oct. 17, 1983, p. 88.

Growth in Sales by Category
(in millions)

	1984	% change from 1982	1982	1972
Textbooks	$2,589.7	18.0%	$2,193.9	$ 872.9
Trade	1,695.8	25.1	1,355.5	444.8
Professional†	1,458.1	18.5	1,230.5	381.0
Book club and mail order	1,234.8	3.4	1,194.6	439.4
Mass market paperbacks*	732.9	10.1	665.5	250.0
Religion	461.7	18.4	390.0	117.5
Other**	948.4	16.5	814.3	512.2
Total	$9,121.4	16.3%	$7,844.3	$3,017.8

† Includes technical, scientific, business and other professional books.
* Rack-size; non-rack-size paperbacks included in trade category.
** Includes university presses, standardized tests, subscription references and audio-visual and other media material.

Source: Association of American Publishers

have not interfered in the editorial decisions of their publishing subsidiaries. "In my 10 years with Gulf & Western," Simon & Schuster head Synder said, "not one G&W manager has ever once suggested what we publish or who we should publish." [24] But others, including Ben Bagdikian, a professor in the graduate school of journalism at the University of California at Berkeley, say that corporate domination over publishing has had a negative impact on editorial policy. "The care with which books generally have been produced has been diluted as editors have suffered lowered status in favor of packagers and promoters," Bagdikian said. "In conglomerate-owned publishing houses, the process is governed as much by the vagaries of the stock market as by those of the book market." [25]

One unarguable impact of mergers and acquisitions has been the closing down of unprofitable publishing houses and the resulting loss of jobs. There also have been instances, Dessauer said, "where a relatively small imprint, which could support comfortably a small establishment, would not throw off the kind of profits that would satisfy a large corporation and be axed — not because it wasn't contributing to doing a good job publishing or because it was not economically viable, but because its levels of profit were not sufficient to satisfy the corporation."

In recent months large corporations have dissolved two established imprints. In April Macmillan announced the end of

[24] Quoted in *U.S. News & World Report,* Dec. 10, 1984, p. 86.
[25] Ben Bagdikian, *The Media Monopoly* (1983), p. 19.

Bobbs-Merrill, a 157-year-old publishing house that once was an important publisher of fiction. After it was purchased by ITT, Bobbs-Merrill shifted to self-help books and cookbooks, a move that turned out to be economically unsuccessful.

Doubleday announced in March that it plans to disband the Dial Press this fall. Founded in 1924, Dial publishes primarily novels; the press numbers among its accomplishments publication of the first unabridged version of D. H. Lawrence's *Lady Chatterly's Lover* in 1944. Doubleday also announced it would reorganize and cut back the number of titles published by Anchor Press. Founded by Doubleday in 1952 Anchor Press specializes in reissuing out-of-print hardcover and quality paperback books. Doubleday President Henry Reath said the decisions to close Dial and scale back Anchor were made for economic reasons.

Some Gaps Filled by Small Publishers

During this period of mergers and acquisitions the number of small, independent publishing houses has increased substantially. Industry sources estimate that as many as 200 new publishers start operations every month, and that the total number of publishing houses — some 20,000 — has quadrupled in the last decade. Not all of them are successful, but scores of small publishers have made an impact in the book publishing world. Among these:

● Ten Speed Press of Berkeley, Calif., began publishing paperbacks on bicycling in 1971 and now puts out about 20 art, cooking, gardening and other books a year. *What Color Is Your Parachute,* a book on how to search for a job, has consistently been a best-seller.

● Meadowbrook Press of Deephaven, Minn., started in 1974, and publishes about a dozen paperback children's books annually.

● Peter Bedrick Books was founded in 1983 in New York City and now has more than 70 books in print, primarily children's books co-published with British publishers.

● North Point Press of Berkeley, Calif., began in 1980 and publishes about 25 books of fiction, poetry and reissued classics, primarily in paperback, annually.

Some industry analysts say the small presses fill some of the gaps left by the big corporations. Small publishers, *Publishers Weekly* Editor in Chief Baker commented, are "able, by reason of their low overhead, to give personal attention to books of literary merit that larger publishers would find uncommercial. . . ." [26] Robert Wilson, *USA Today's* book editor, said that an unusually large number of good writers are being published

---

[26] Baker, *op. cit.,* p. 30.

today by small presses, including North Point. "They have a publicity and promotion and advertising staff of one person," Wilson said of North Point, "And they just had their first best-seller, *Son of the Morning Star* by Evan Connell."

But others say that the growth of small houses does not mean that more high-quality books are being published. "As soon as two old ladies in Florida start a company in order to produce a cookbook, the Association of American Publishers quickly say, 'Aha, there's another publisher,'" Roger Straus, president of Farrar, Straus & Giroux, said five years ago during a debate on the issue. "But the fact of the matter is, there are fewer publishers in the middle line than there ever were before. And as this happens, as the pressure comes from the owners of these companies each year to produce 6 percent more profit than last year, then those books are being put to one side and aren't being published. And I think it's very bad for literature." [27]

A special segment of small publishing is the university press. The nation's 125 university presses account for about 5,000 — some 10 percent — of all book titles published annually but for only about 1 percent of all books sold. Most university press books, such as multi-volume editions of the letters, journals and public papers of prominent literary, political and military figures, appeal to narrow audiences. Many university presses are, funded by endowments, but they are also dependent on library sales and have been affected by funding cuts in library budgets.

Scholarly books "are hurt mainly because the libraries don't have enough money to buy them," David H. Gilber, director of the University of Nebraska Press, said. "As a result, we shorten our press runs, and as you do, your unit costs go up. It creates a difficult spiral effect, and that ... is our key economic problem." [28]

To survive economically, many university presses have augmented their scholarly works with books of more general interest, including fiction. The University of Nebraska Press, for example, has published paperback reprints of the works of Nebraska native Willa Cather. Harvard University Press published novelist Eudora Welty's autobiographical *One Writer's Beginnings* in 1984. The book made *The New York Times* nonfiction best-seller list, and became the first best-seller published by Harvard University Press in its 71-year history. Another recent university press best-seller was *A Confederacy of Dunces*, a novel by John Kennedy O'Toole, which was pub-

---

[27] Appearing on PBS-TV's "The MacNeil/Lehrer Report," May 2, 1980.
[28] Quoted in *The New York Times*, April 20, 1984.

lished posthumously in 1980 by Louisiana State University Press and won that year's Pulitzer Prize for fiction.[29]

Questions of Quality

E XCEPT FOR the handful of writers who turn out million-selling books with regularity, writing books is not the easiest way to make a living. A survey commissioned by the Author's Guild in 1979 indicated that 31 percent of full-time authors in virtually every field of fact and fuction earned less than $5,000 a year from writing and that two-thirds did not make as much as $20,000 annually. The survey, which was conducted by Columbia University's Center for the Social Sciences, also found that only 10 percent of the authors had annual incomes of $45,000 or more. Peter Heggie, the guild's executive director, said that the situation has not changed markedly, although "dollar amounts might have climbed the ladder a bit compared with inflation."

The 1979 survey found that nearly half of all professional authors worked in other jobs to supplement their writing income. "I advise virtually every author I work with to make sure he has a full-time job doing something else," Harold Roth said. "I always tell them to be like [17th-century Dutch philosopher Baruch] Spinoza, who wrote his philosophy in his spare time and who worked as a lens grinder most of the week. The odds against you really making it as a writer are high."

Some of the authors who have made it have serious complaints about the "MBAism" of today's trade publishing giants. Authors and agents say that trade publishing opportunities have shrunk because of the closing down of imprints and publishers' emphasis on best-sellers. Others say the 50,000 books published each year are evidence that there are more opportunities for authors than ever before. "It would be hard to argue that authors in this country are threatened and that their chances of being published are diminished," Dessauer said. "I haven't seen any evidence of that."

Roth and Irwin Karp, counsel to the Author's Guild, disagreed. Roth said that best-selling authors seem to be doing as well as ever, but that others are having trouble. "The hot best-sellers are still just as hot — maybe they even sell more than

---

[29] O'Toole had committed suicide several years before after several publishers rejected his manuscript.

Literacy Worries

The latest survey of book-reading habits indicates that reading among young persons has fallen off alarmingly in recent years. Sixty-three percent of those 21 and younger said they read books — compared with 75 percent of that age group who said they read books in 1978. Although adult readership was up slightly, only 39 percent of persons 60 years old and older surveyed said they were book readers, compared with 56 percent of the population as a whole.*

The reading survey did not address a parallel issue, the growing problem of illiteracy. Experts believe that anywhere from 25 million to 60 million American adults either cannot read or have only the barest reading skills. They also warn that the number of illiterate Americans is growing by more than two million a year.

Marginally and functionally illiterate people "cannot read enough to understand the poison warnings on a can of pesticide or the antidote instructions on a can of kitchen lye, nor can they understand the warnings of the sedative effects of non-prescription drugs, handle a checking account, read editorials in a newspaper, nor read the publications of the U.S. Census, which persists in telling us with stubborn, jingoistic pride that 99.4 percent of all Americans can read and write," Jonathan Kozol, author of *Illiterate America*, wrote in the May 24, 1985, edition of *Publishers Weekly*.

The high rate of illiteracy is, of course, of primary importance to book publishers. Aside from the illiterate themselves, "book industry members should be expected to feel [the impact of illiteracy] most acutely," an editorial in that same *Publishers Weekly* commented. ". . . [A] literate public is a sine qua non for publishers, booksellers and other book industry members. . . ."

The book industry is working on several fronts to help solve the problem of illiteracy. B. Dalton Bookseller, a leading bookstore chain, recently inaugurated a $3 million program that provides grants to literacy programs nationwide, and several regional bookseller organizations are involved in similar programs. Various individual publishers, including Penguin Books, New American Library, Bantam Books, Acropolis Books, Jalmar Press and Doubleday, have set up programs to promote literacy.

Some believe that publishers could do even more. "I don't think [book publishers] have all been sufficiently aware of the dimensions of the problem," said Harold McGraw, chairman of McGraw-Hill Inc. and founder of the Business Council for Effective Literacy. "A number of publishers have come out with low-vocabulary, high-interest books and some of these have been geared to adults. But more such books are needed. Publishers have also brought out books on illiteracy. But most of us say: 'We've got a business to run. . . .' "

* *The survey, which was commissioned by the Book Industry Study Group and released April 11, 1984, was conducted in 1983 and updated a similar 1978 project.*

they ever did before," Roth said. "But the middle book and the sort of marginal [selling] bottom-list book are having bigger problems than ever before." Roth said that publishers are increasingly reluctant to publish books that do not sell large quantities rapidly. "There are so many new books coming out so fast that if a book doesn't catch on immediately, it gets returned [by the bookseller to the publisher] almost instantaneously, instead of sitting around and maybe aging and getting a chance to develop its own market," Roth said.

Karp said that book agents "continually talk about how much more difficult it is to place the middle-range book — a book by a competent, established author" that is unlikely to become a best-seller. Karp noted "a great increase" in the number of books publishers reject under "satisfactory manuscript" clauses and in the number of instances publishers ask authors to accept lower royalty rates. These actions, Karp said, "are to some extent due to this concentration of power and the greater and greater intensity with which people in publishing focus on the bottom line."

Influence of Chains on Book Availability

There also has been a concentration of power in recent years in the nation's bookselling industry. Books are sold at some 20,000 retail outlets in this country, an increase of about 3,000 in the last three years. That total includes airport newsstands, drugstores, department stores and any other venue that sells books. The American Booksellers Association estimates that there are about 9,500 full-line bookstores.

About 80 percent of these are independently owned. But bookselling is in many ways dominated by the four large chains that own the other 20 percent: Waldenbooks (with 920 stores), B. Dalton Bookseller (734 stores), Barnes & Noble (92) and Crown Books (183). Waldenbooks, owned by K Mart, led all the chains in 1984 revenue with $491 million, a yearly increase of 17.2 percent, according to data compiled by the newsletter, *BP Report*. B. Dalton had $489.9 million in revenue; Barnes and Noble, $155 million and Crown, $114.4 million.

Barnes & Noble and Crown are discount chains. Crown, which is owned by Dart Corp. and Thrifty Drug, has grown rapidly since it was started in 1977. In some areas small, independent booksellers unable to compete with Crown's discounting policy have gone out of business. "A typical independent gets a 40-45 percent discount, presuming he buys at least 20 copies of a book," said Commerce Department publishing analyst William Lofquist. "The chain will buy 20,000 copies and get volume discounts [of 50 percent]." Some independents, as well as the non-discounting chains, have fought back by discounting a few books, typically hardcover best-sellers. Others emphasize personal service or specialize in certain types of books such as children's or business books.

Some in the publishing industry are concerned that the large chains have too much influence on what gets published. There is "no question," the authors of a 1983 book on publishing wrote, "that chains emphasize books with fast turnover. Many wholesalers note that chains are restrictive in title selection, favoring best-sellers and category titles to the exclusion of back-list books." [30] In other words, the chains tend to reserve shelf space for guaranteed best-sellers by name authors, books that are hot at the moment (such as celebrity exercise books or diet books) and low-cost sale books called remainders.[31] Many books that have been published in the recent past and sell in steady but low quantities, are difficult, if not impossible, to find at the discount chains.

The ability of the large chains virtually to assure the success of a big-name author's latest book or a popular genre of book "may lend itself to ... formula publishing," Lofquist said. "Let's say how-to books are selling well in Waldens, especially how-to books on Oriental cooking. Very soon all the big publishers are coming out with how-to Oriental cookbooks."

Industry analysts expect that the number of new titles published annually will stay around 50,000 and that authors of high-quality fiction and non-fiction will continue to go unrecognized, even unpublished. "Some of our greatest artists and writers are not going to find a ready market," Dessauer said, "because they don't please whatever literary or cultural mafia happens to be disposing of taste at the time or they happen to be so far out, literally, that the world hasn't caught up to them yet."

But there is little concern that the popularity of personal computers and videocassette recorders will eventually make book reading — and publishing — obsolete. "There will always be a need for book publishing," Roth said. "There will always be a need for books. Books represent the last individual activity known to mankind. You don't have a machine you have to work; you can read when you want to and stop when you want to. You can do a lot of things without the intervention of machines or anything mechanical." And, Roth said, there always will be authors: "The creative impulse can't be stopped; people will continue to write no matter what."

---

[30] Lewis A. Coser, *et al.*, *Books: The Culture and Commerce of Publishing* (1982), p. 353.
[31] Unsold hardcover books are returned to publishers for refunds by bookstores. Often publishers sell those returns at exceedingly low prices to wholesalers, who offer the books — which are called remainders — to bookstores at greatly reduced prices.

Selected Bibliography

Books

Adler, Bill, *Inside Publishing*, Bobbs-Merrill, 1982.
Bagdikian, Ben H., *The Media Monopoly*, Beacon Press, 1983.
Bailey, Herbert S. Jr., *The Art and Science of Book Publishing*, University of Texas Press, 1980.
Book Publishing Annual: Highlights, Analyses & Trends, 1984 edition, R.R. Bowker, 1984.
Coser, Lewis A., et. al., *Books: The Culture and Commerce of Publishing*, Basic Books, 1982.
Crider, Allen Billy, *Mass Market Publishing in America*, G.K. Hall, 1982.
Davis, Kenneth C., *Two-Bit Culture*, Houghton Mifflin, 1984.
Dessauer, John P., *Book Publishing: What It Is, What It Does*, R.R. Bowker, 1981.
Duke, Judith S., ed., *The Knowledge Industry 200: America's Two Hundred Largest Media Companies, 1983*, Knowledge Industries, 1984.
Grannis, Chandler B., ed., *What Happens in Book Publishing*, 2nd ed., Columbia University Press, 1967.
Knopf, Alfred A., *Publishing Then and Now: 1912-1964*, New York Public Library, 1964.
Tebbel, John, *A History of Book Publishing in the United States*, 4 vols., R.R. Bowker, 1972, 1975, 1978, 1981.
Weybright, Victor, *The Making of A Publisher*, Reynal, 1966.
Whiteside, Thomas, *The Blockbuster Complex*, Wesleyan University Press, 1981.

Articles

BP Report: On the Business of Book Publishing, Knowledge Industry Publications, selected issues.
Publishers Weekly, selected issues.
Sanoff, Alvin P., "Behind Merger Mania in Book Publishing," *U.S. News & World Report*, Dec. 10, 1984.

Reports and Studies

Book Industry Study Group, "The 1983 Consumer Research Study on Reading and Book Purchasing," April 11, 1984; "Book Industry Trends, 1984," 1985.
Editorial Research Reports: "Illiteracy in America," 1983 Vol. I, p. 473; "Schoolbook Controversies," 1982 Vol. II, p. 673; "Book Publishing," 1975 Vol. II, p. 327.
"LMP, 1984: Literary Market Place: The Directory of American Book Publishing," R.R. Bowker, 1983.
"U.S. Industrial Outlook, 1985," U.S. Department of Commerce, 1985.

Graphics: Art Director Richard Pottern and Staff Artist Kathleen Ossenfort.

TRENDS IN ARCHITECTURE

by

Jean Rosenblatt

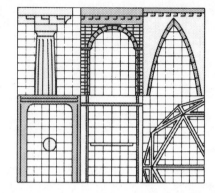

Jan. 22
1 9 8 2

TRENDS IN ARCHITECTURE

A LONG WITH television and the printed word, architecture is one of the most pervasive forces in our lives. Although architects design only about 3 percent of all new single-family houses in the United States, they do design the public buildings, parks, apartment houses, office buildings and shopping centers that form the scenery along city streets and highways. Since World War II this scenery has become largely a wall of glass boxes that neither expand our vision — one traditional view of architecture's goal — nor give any hint of the activity going on inside. But lately that scene has begun to change.

"The art of architecture is in uneasy but significant transition," critic Ada Louise Huxtable wrote in *The New York Review of Books*. "The high period of modernism is over; the Age of the Masters — Frank Lloyd Wright, Mies van der Rohe, Le Corbusier — is finished." [1] Replacing the sterile-looking glass, steel and concrete structures of modern architecture — a style that emerged in the 1920s and emphasized man's relationship to machinery and technology — is a style closer to what architects call "the human scale." Philip Johnson, whom many regard as the dean of American architects, described the new generation of architects who began surfacing in the 1970s: "We have new attitudes today, a new pluralism, a new belief in many streams flowing at once. There are no certitudes today. And we have a new willingness to use history, to use symbols — we don't want everything to look like a glass box anymore." [2]

The new look, which is really many new looks, has been called "post-modernism" and incorporates historical references (what many see as a romantic or even humorous approach to design), a variety of deviations from the box form, and the idea that a building should be related to its site and use. Post-modernism "recognizes that buildings are designed to mean something, that they are not hermetically sealed objects...," architect Robert A. M. Stern wrote in *New Directions in American Architecture* (1977). "Post-modernism accepts diversity; it prefers hybrids to pure forms; it encourages multiple and simultaneous readings in its effort to heighten expressive content." [3]

[1] *The New York Review of Books,* July 16, 1981, p. 17.
[2] Quoted in *The New York Times,* May 29, 1978.
[3] Robert A. M. Stern, *New Directions in American Architecture* (1977), pp. 134, 135.

Model of Piazza d'Italia designed by Charles W. Moore

A structure that illustrates these principles is Charles W. Moore's Piazza d'Italia, built in New Orleans in the late 1970s *(see photo, above)*. The piazza was commissioned by a group of Italian-Americans to embellish the forecourt of an undistinguished office tower and evokes old Italian monuments as well as Hollywood's version of them. According to Huxtable, it "offers classical recall seen through a sophisticated Pop eye at the same time that it is turned into something totally unlike its traditional sources for a collage of academic references, colors, and symbols — plus neon." [4]

Emergence of the 'Glass Box' Design

It was a man named Walter Gropius who set the style for architectural design that became known as modernism. In 1919, in the German capital Weimar, he founded the Bauhaus School and set out to glorify the machine and technology using the motto "art and technology — the new unity" as a guiding principle. Another architect working in the 1920s, and perhaps the most influential, was Le Corbusier (Charles Edouard Jeanneret). He called the houses he designed "machines for living" and was best known for his radical ideas about mass housing, which involved stripping away all ornamentation and reducing buildings to pure, functional form.

But it wasn't until after World War II that the International Style — a term coined in 1932 by Philip Johnson, then curator

---

[4] Ada Louise Huxtable, "The Troubled State of Modern Architecture," *Architectural Record*, January 1981, p. 77.

of the Museum of Modern Art — came into its own. The

International Style, which eventually became known simply as modern architecture, was, according to *New York Times* architecture critic Paul Goldberger, "conceived in the 1920s as a utopian architecture that would break dramatically with the historic styles of the past.... But its stark lines and austere esthetic were widely adopted not so much as a symbol of a brave new age — as its creators had envisioned it — than as a way of quickly erecting cheap buildings at a time when craftsmanship was dying." By the 1950s, Goldberger wrote, "the glass box, envisioned in the 1920s as a physical shelter for a new, socialist society, became the architecture of corporate capitalism."

One of the best known glass towers erected in the 1950s is the Seagram Building in New York City, designed by Mies van der Rohe and Philip Johnson. At the time the brightness of its glass walls seemed to open up the dense and closed city, but it also bred a number of bad imitations. "As New York and most other American cities filled up in the 1960s with poorly wrought, cheap imitations of Seagram, it became clear that what had looked so good when new and unusual

Photo by Alexandre Georges

Seagram Building

looked wretched when old and common," Goldberger wrote. "It also became clear that glass boxes alone could not a city make: They were too thin, too cold, too lacking in emotion to form the solid and coherent unity that older, masonry buildings possessed." [5]

In *The Language of Post-Modern Architecture,* architect Charles Jencks traces the death of modern architecture to an afternoon in St. Louis on July 15, 1972, when parts of the Pruitt-Igoe housing project were blown up by the city after they had been vandalized beyond repair. The Pruitt-Igoe had won an award when it was designed in 1951 and consisted of slab blocks 14 stories high. Its design included "streets in the air," which were free of cars, as intended, but not of crime. "Its Purist style,

[5] Paul Goldberger, "The New American Skyscraper," *The New York Times Magazine,* Nov. 8, 1981, p. 76.

145

its clean, salubrious hospital metaphor, was meant to instill, by good example, corresponding virtues in its inhabitants," Jencks wrote.[6] But the crime rate was higher in the Pruitt-Igoe than in other developments, a fact that Jencks and others have attributed to the long corridors, anonymity of the buildings and lack of controlled semi-private space. According to Jencks, the building was designed in a purist style totally at odds with its inhabitants.

Forces Shaping Architecture's New Look

Among the forces shaping architecture today, according to David O. Meeker, executive vice president of the American Institute of Architects (AIA), in Washington, D.C., is the likelihood that about 80 percent of all buildings now standing will be here through the turn of the century. This, combined with rapidly rising land prices, makes the renovation of older buildings a significant architectural trend — not only an attractive investment for owners but also an interesting challenge to architects, Meeker said in a recent interview. Public policy, expressed in tax terms, also encourages renovation of old buildings. The 1981 Economic Recovery Act provides up to a 25 percent tax credit for historic preservation of buildings as well as write-off opportunities for rehabilitation of buildings over 30 years old.

Demographics is another factor influencing architecture. "The fact that the percentage of people 55 and older in our population is the most rapidly growing portion will mean that their needs, perceptions and ambitions will contribute more and more to what architecture has to provide, both in terms of its accessibility and physical appearance," Meeker said. Experts believe that people in this age group are more attracted to buildings that are warmer in feeling and more romantic- and solid-looking than the stark glass and steel that have dominated building styles since World War II. Architectural experts see a growing nostalgia and desire to identify with the past among other age groups, as well, which will influence architecture as much as it has influenced fashion and interior design.

The demand for affordable housing by the "baby boomers" now in their mid-twenties through mid-thirties has already begun to influence the design of single-family houses. Houses will continue to shrink in size[7] and will be more expandable and made up of more essentials with fewer luxuries. Rising energy costs have much to do with this trend, and architects are now concentrating more than ever on finding design solutions to energy-related problems *(see p. 154).*

---

[6] Charles A. Jencks, *The Language of Post-Modern Architecture* (1977), p. 9.
[7] The average single-family home built in 1980 had 1,595 square feet of living space, down from a decade high of 1,655 in 1978.

Elements of Post-Modernism

F OR INCREASING numbers of architects and their clients, old is in. At a hearing before the Senate Committee on Appropriations on March 26, 1981, a spokesman for the American Institute of Architects predicted that 77 percent of all construction activity that year would probably involve "preservation, adaptive use and renovation" of old buildings. Recycling of buildings accounted for more architectural income in 1980 than any other source — more than $40 million. Architects predict that in the 1980s they will be working as much with renovation as with creating new designs.

"Renovation used to be strictly second-class work," said Hugh Hardy, of Hardy Holzman Pfeiffer Associates (HHPA), a team of restorers who received one of AIA's highest awards in 1981. "Now it's a serious, first-class matter." [8] Most top architects, as well as the lesser known, are now engaged in restoration and are touching on just about every past architectural style. Philip Johnson, for example — once a devout modernist — recently designed a facade for a Fifth Avenue apartment house that imitates nearby moldings designed in 1911. In Washington, D.C., HHPA is restoring the famous Willard Hotel on Pennsylvania Avenue. In addition to cleaning and repainting the old facade and the main reception and dining rooms and building a new wing, the firm may use its trademark of exposed, brightly-colored pipes beneath the ceiling. This kind of wry mixing of the old and new is not uncommon among architects working in restoration. In their conversion of an old Baptist church in Charlotte, N.C., to an arts center, HHPA used a marble baptismal font for a theater box office.

Victorian architecture is one of many references to the past receiving a lot of attention, but preservation is not always the reason behind Victorian-inspired designs. The Victorian theme of Washington, D.C.'s ornate new shopping mall, Georgetown Park, was chosen "to identify with the existing architecture and human scale of Georgetown," said Phillip Ross of the Western Development Corp., which, with Conohoe Companies, developed the project. Georgetown Park comes replete with pressed tin ceilings, patterned tile floors, beveled-leaded-glass transoms, hand-cast lighting fixtures, cast-iron railings made from century-old molds and a large stone fountain decorated with antique gold leaf — details designed to evoke the Victorian period (1837-1901) by reinterpreting it rather than recreating it literally.

---

[8] Quoted in "Restoration of Things Past," *Newsweek*, March 23, 1981, p. 84.

Victorian architecture actually refers to several different styles that themselves were conscious reinterpretations of earlier styles such as Gothic and Romanesque. Gothic Revival is characterized by steeply pitched roofs, pointed arches and gingerbread trim; Romanesque Revival is known for its towers and semicircular arched windows; Italianate incorporates rectangular shapes, wide eaves and low-pitched roofs; and Queen Anne is an asymmetrical style using towers, porches, bay projections and textured surfaces.

Many architects are designing what they call modern Victorian houses that include light wood floors, white walls and plenty of windows, along with 19th-century-inspired high ceilings, archways, bay windows, stained glass, steeply pitched roofs and turrets. That people are choosing to build and revive homes in this expensive style is evidence that Victorian architecture may become a trend. Dr. Richard Howland, president of the Victorian Society in America (in Philadelphia) and special assistant to the Secretary of the Smithsonian Institution in Washington, D.C., said of Georgetown Park: "If some big business is willing to invest so much money in a project like that, then it seems the Victorian revival is here to stay." [9] Other evidence supports this conclusion. Schumacher, a well-known fabric and wallpaper manufacturer, recently introduced a line of Victorian fabrics and wallpapers, and some plaster studios have doubled the number of Victorian moldings and ceiling medallions they offer.

The irony of the revival of 19th-century architecture is that it was originally rejected for the clean lines of the International Style. Now the ornateness and warmth of Victoriana are seen as offering relief from the coldness of many modern houses. Social critic Tom Wolfe wrote of this type of house: "I once saw the owners of such a place driven to the edge of sensory deprivation by the whiteness & lightness & leanness & cleanness & bareness & spareness of it all. They became desperate for an antidote, such as coziness & color." [10]

New Buildings Related to Their Context

What architects call contextualism is a fundamental principle of post-modernism. This simply means that a building is viewed as a fragment of a larger whole, whether it be related to its purpose, the physical site — including the buildings adjacent to it — or the social and cultural milieu in which it is built. The TWA building at Kennedy Airport in New York and the Dulles

---

[9] Quoted by Elizabeth Sporkin in "Victoriana Is Back," *The Washingtonian*, December 1981, p. 232.
[10] Tom Wolfe, "From Bauhaus To Our House," *Harper's*, June 1981, p. 33.

Airport passenger terminal in Virginia, both designed by Eero Saarinen, are examples of buildings that communicate their purpose — flight — in their form and design.

New York architect Romaldo Giurgola, recipient of the 1982 gold medal awarded by the American Institute of Architects,[11] is in the forefront of those trying to integrate buildings with the land- and cityscape. "Mr. Giurgola does not build glass boxes...," Paul Goldberger wrote. "In almost all his work, the shapes and lines that constitute a building's form emerge from, or try to respond to, the physical surroundings of that building — the nearby streets, the forms of adjacent buildings and the like."[12] Giurgola himself has written: "A building is a fragment of the larger environment, which includes other continuously growing structures and the natural scape. The point of architecture is to unfold and formulate a relationship often hidden between elements and the events that make an environment."

Thorncrown Chapel in Eureka Springs, Ark. *(see photo, p. 150)*, recipient of a 1981 AIA award, incorporates many of these principles. The firm that designed the building, Fay Jones & Associates Architects, describes it as a kind of reversal of Gothic cathedral architecture, which has repeated external flying buttresses pushing the structure upward and inward. In a statement about how the chapel's site determined its design, the architects wrote: "In walking the eight-acre wooded hillside site, there was an early realization that heavy earth-moving equipment or massive construction materials could not be used without destroying the wooded setting and that the whole design must hinge on not using anything too big for two men to carry along a narrow hillside pathway. This limitation was the key to the structural concept." The solution was to cut, assemble and tilt the structural wood frames into place at the site. Native stone walls support and anchor the frame, which was handrubbed with a grayish stain to blend in with the bark of the surrounding trees and the stone base. In summer the wooded setting and broad roof overhangs help cool the chapel, which is used very little during cold months.

A city street forms the context of a building more often than a wooded hillside but can pose just as many problems. Most architects agree that the design of a new building should complement its older neighbors rather than simply make its own statement. The design of a Washington, D.C., office building illustrates how this is planned for a street with two old brick schools — the 109-year-old Sumner School on 17th Street and

---

[11] The award is presented in recognition of "most distinguished service to the architectural profession or to the institute."
[12] Writing in *The New York Times*, Jan. 3, 1982.

Thorncrown Chapel, Eureka Springs, Ark.

its neighbor around the corner on M Street, the 94-year-old Magruder School. The design by Warren Cox and George Hartman places the bulk of the new building behind and to the sides of the two older buildings, placing them, in effect, on a framed platform. In an attempt to make the new building as invisible as possible, the architects propose to sheathe the upper floors, which will tower above the older buildings, with a mirror-glass curtain wall that from street level will reflect only sky. The lower floors will be sheathed in glass of a darker hue, to form an unobtrusive backdrop for one of the schools. The wings of the new building will, according to one of the architects, "mirror the facades of their next-door neighbors," mimicking their window designs and brick and stone textured surfaces. According to critic Benjamin Forgey of *The Washington Post*, the design by Hartman and Cox provides "a vigorous, thought-provoking re-introduction to the potential civility of the city street." [13]

---

[13] Writing in *The Washington Post*, Dec. 5, 1981

Another effort to juxtapose the old and the new does not seem to be working as well in New York City, where a proposed new building has generated considerable controversy. St. Bartholomew's Episcopal Church — a Byzantine church built in 1919 and recently seen in the movie "Arthur" — sits on the east blockfront of Park Avenue between 50th and 51st Streets. It is on the last piece of land on Park Avenue not occupied by commercial real estate, a site affording a rare bit of light and sky in a dense and overcrowded part of midtown Manhattan.

Church members have voted to sell off some of the land for the construction of a 59-story skyscraper, which would mean tearing down the St. Bartholomew Community House, a city landmark adjacent to the church. The church wants the millions of dollars that would come from the sale for missionary work. But leaders in urban preservation, including Jacqueline Kennedy Onassis, are up in arms about the proposed project and have said they will continue to fight the sale in court. The church has accepted a plan for a tower of mirrored glass intended to reflect the church's dome and the masonry walls of the surrounding buildings, including the Waldorf-Astoria Hotel. The facade of the community house would be saved and tacked onto the front of the tower's base. The plan for the tower itself calls for a many-sided skyscraper with setbacks at the top and a sequence of zigzags projecting outward toward the dome.

Many of New York's finest architects have refused to have anything to do with the plan, which *New York Times* architecture critic Paul Goldberger labeled in a front-page story as the wrong building for the wrong place. He called the attempt to preserve the integrity of St. Bartholomew's with mirrors a "gross and awkward" solution, "an intrusion of glittering glass into a grouping of buildings noted for their masonry quality." [14] Cesar Pelli, dean of the School of Architecture at Princeton, has called the St. Bartholomew plan a disaster. Philip Johnson commented: "It would be preferable to tear the church down. They have been very clever to do the proper kinds of renderings so it will not look overpowering, but clearly the building will hang over the dome. To overhang a church is to kill it. Can you imagine erecting a glass tower over St. Peter's?" [15]

Skyscrapers Built in Variety of Shapes

The battle over St. Bartholomew's glass tower is occurring amid a renaissance of skyscraper building and design in American cities. Architects seem to be setting skylines aflame with lively new shapes, and clients evidently are willing to go along.

[14] Writing in *The New York Times*, Oct. 30, 1981.
[15] Quoted by Marie Brenner, "Holy War on Park Avenue," *New York*, Dec. 14, 1981, p. 41.

"The meeting of a building with the sky is a very important event," said Cesar Pelli. "It must be celebrated." [16] Ground has just been broken for a group of office buildings by Pelli whose "roof tops and upper floors [were] consciously designed to create a special and interesting effect," according to the developer.

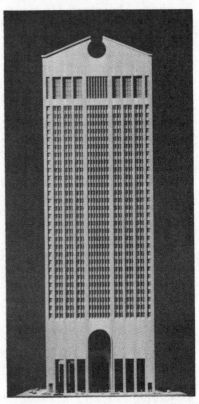

Photo by Hedrich Blessing
Model of A.T.&T. Corporate Headquarters

Perhaps the most famous celebration so far is the granite tower designed by Philip Johnson and John Burgee for the American Telephone & Telegraph Co. on Madison Avenue in New York City, the showplace of American architecture's new flamboyance. The AT&T building features a "Chippendale" broken-pediment top and a Renaissance-inspired base. When the design was announced in 1978 it caused an uproar from architects and the public alike. Johnson and Burgee were accused of everything from trying to turn back history to designing nothing but a large Chippendale bureau.

Other variations from the modernist mold include Cesar Pelli's tower for the Museum of Modern Art, with a "setback" top and patterned "skin" (surface) of colored glass; the Trump Tower on Fifth Avenue in New York, with its tiny setbacks and zigzags all the way up its 58 stories;[17] the curved Xerox Center in Chicago that will look like it just rolled out of a machine; and the IBM tower in New York, which will have a greenhouse-like public park at its base and be sheathed in dark green granite to give it a look of permanence. According to Paul Goldberger, the AT&T building, the Trump Tower and the IBM building, all being built within a single block, each represents different aspects of the current generation's developing style. One aspect is the historical esthetic, illustrated by the AT&T building, in

[16] Quoted by Carter Wiseman in "Room at the Tops," *New York*, Dec. 21, 1981, p. 65.
[17] The tower's chief designer, Der Scutt, has said his architectural goal was to create lively forms that will bring pleasure to the public.

which architects either copy past styles or reinterpret historical forms. The Trump Tower represents a move toward sculptured form for its own sake, while the IBM building evokes what Goldberger labels "the esthetic of a post-mechanical age, in which the machines are computers that make no noise and conceal their inner workings." [18]

Although they point to many bad examples, in general most critics seem to be pleased by the variety of post-modern forms and styles cropping up on cities' skylines. But Ada Louise Huxtable is disturbed by what she sees as "an eclecticism that does no more than exploit history as a grab-bag of ideas for surface spectacle." It is possible, she claims, that the "new" architecture is another version of an if-it-feels-good-do-it type of mentality in which architects ignore the basic relationships involved in structure, form, style and use. "I think that what is deeply disturbing is a philosophy of building so superficial that the only thing that matters is how one expands the visual boundaries of design," Huxtable wrote. "With every other kind of response downgraded, this approach can produce a lot of very bad building, very fast." [19]

Impact of Zoning Laws on Architecture

Along with all the excitement over the current rejuvenation in urban architecture has come basic questions about city planning. Architecture, whether good or bad, may not matter much if cities are so crowded their inhabitants can barely see the sky. When New York City's zoning ordinance was adopted in 1916 (the first comprehensive ordinance in the United States), it sought to preserve sunlight and air by limiting how high a tower could rise from the street before stepping back. Zoning, therefore, was partly responsible for the setback style of the 1920s — the golden age of New York skyscrapers — now coming back into vogue.

By 1961 Manhattan streets had become so dense with buildings that the New York zoning ordinance began encouraging the creation of plazas to open up street-level space. Buildings could rise straight up without setbacks if they occupied only 40 or 50 percent of the property. In the late 1960s, zoning laws began to offer incentives to preserve certain types of buildings, ones that gave character to particular districts, such as theaters in Times Square and stores on Fifth Avenue. In the mid-1970s atriums, often just lobbies with waterfalls, became the favored space. And according to Suzanne Stephens, editor of *Skyline* magazine, "the attitude has shifted once again. Sunlight and open-

---

[18] Goldberger, *The New York Times Magazine, op. cit.,* p. 92.
[19] Column published in *The New York Times,* May 13, 1979.

ness outside are again valued; yet it is too late to get back what is lost. The real question is, can zoning assure that those qualities of the environment held in esteem by its citizens will in fact be preserved?" [20]

The New York City Planning Department recently proposed revisions of the city's zoning laws based on a report it published in June on the revamping of midtown Manhattan's zoning regulations.[21] According to Stephens, the department's recommendations would encourage buildings that preserve daylight and openness, thereby acknowledging a pedestrian's perception of buildings rather than only the typical aerial view. But Stephens believes most low-rise buildings in midtown Manhattan will disappear unless they are declared landmarks or occupy specially designated blocks. In the end, Stephens gloomily predicts, not only will the sky be increasingly less visible because of overbuilding, but also "there will still be many badly designed, boring-looking towers, just with some slightly new shapes."

Energy as Design Influence

AROUND the time of World War II mechanical systems, including air conditioning units that regulated air flow, became an important part of architecture and made it possible to create indoor climates without regard to what went on outside. The problem was that these systems gobbled enormous amounts of energy. Residential and commercial energy use in this country nearly tripled between 1950 and 1973.[22] Lighting levels in buildings also increased in the 1950s and 1960s, and builders continued to use single-pane windows and minimal insulation.

When the energy crisis struck in the early 1970s Americans first responded defensively by turning down thermostats and putting in storm windows. But now architects — notoriously slow to change their ways — are taking a more active stance.

---

[20] Suzanne Stephens, "The Sky is not the Limit: Midtown Zoning," *Skyline*, October 1981, p. 7. *Skyline* is published by the Institute for Architecture and Urban Studies in New York City.

[21] The legislation has gone through community and borough planning board hearings and will be reviewed by the City Planning Commission in March and voted on by the Board of Estimate in April or May.

[22] See Christopher Flavin, "Energy and Architecture: The Solar and Conservation Potential," Worldwatch Institute, 1980. Worldwatch Institute is a non-profit research organization in Washington, D.C.

They have begun to realize that a building's design can keep energy costs down, a task they had previously left to engineers. That the purpose of the AIA's annual convention last May was to examine ways to conserve energy through architectural design is evidence that energy consciousness among architects is gaining momentum. "Energy has the potential to change the character of the built environment, the potential to create a new vocabulary for design," commented AIA's immediate past-president, R. Randall Vosbeck. "It may be more revolutionary than anything that has happened in architecture since the Renaissance."

One architectural solution to the high price of fuel is to adapt buildings to local, or regional characteristics. This solution is not new; before World War II houses frequently corresponded to a region's climate, lifestyle and availability of materials. For example, Cape Cod houses had long roofs facing north to protect against cold north winds and small windows for keeping in the heat. In contrast, Georgia homes had high ceilings to allow warm air to rise, tall windows to ease air flow through the house and porches that gave shade. Such cost-effective design strategies are coming back in style. "Today," wrote Christopher Flavin in a 1980 report on energy and architecture, "well-designed climate-sensitive buildings that use the sun's energy directly to heat the interior and provide light and that use natural breezes for cooling are reducing fuel bills by 75 to 100 percent, depending on the local climate." [23]

Houses in the Southeast are once more being built with tall windows and porches. Southwestern builders are using adobe and masonry instead of air conditioning to cool houses. Adobe also saves energy by absorbing the sun's heat and then releasing it slowly as the temperature drops. In the Pacific Northwest designers are putting broad overhangs on windows so they can be opened in rainy weather. [24]

But while regional character will be more evident in an area's buildings, new technology will not allow literal imitation of past regional styles, experts say. "It's tough to keep a Colonial house looking Colonial and adding a solar design," said Walter Richardson, an architect in Newport Beach, Calif. [25] Many architects are trying to blend old, traditional styles well adapted to a particular climate with new ideas. Other houses are less traditional in style but still rely on design to solve energy problems.

---

[23] *Ibid.*, p. 6.
[24] According to the AIA there are at least 16 climatic regions in the United States.
[25] Quoted in *The Wall Street Journal*, April 22, 1981.

Crowell House in Vermont

Crowell House in eastern Vermont, near the Green Mountains *(see photo, above),* for example, has a deep sod roof with 18 inches of earth on top. Its only exposed wall faces south, allowing the sun to heat it in fall, winter and spring. The porch roof gives shade in the summer and centers on a decorated gable. The rear walls, set deep into the earth, which remains 50 degrees even in the coldest weather, are concrete and insulated on their outside surfaces. Thus the house is well insulated by wall and earth and can store heat from day to night. Two wood stoves provide a backup heating system. Skylights allow the house, which was designed by Mark Simon, to stay cool and dry in summer and provide ventilation.

Robert Campbell, architect and architecture critic for the *Boston Globe,* is skeptical about the effectiveness of what he calls the popular-science responses to the energy crisis such as earth-sheltered houses and solar panels. "Architects, being visual people, will tend to use the energy crisis to make fancy forms, so you get these underground houses," he told Editorial Research Reports. "There's nothing wrong with them, but they're not going to solve the problem.... Building buildings that are responsive to their sites and to the climate — regardless of how it is done — is more important than any of the energy fixes that make good publicity."

New Climate-Sensitive Office Buildings

One of the major frontiers in climate-sensitive design today is improving the energy characteristics of large office buildings. "In large structures," Flavin explained in his report on energy and architecture, "designs that solve one energy problem can easily aggravate others, and integrating passive heating, cooling, and lighting into the same building requires complicated models, computer programs, and numerous trade-offs. In addition, most large buildings have mechanical systems to control the building's internal environment, and, while these can be made smaller in passive solar buildings, they cannot be eliminated. Energy-efficient design must therefore be integrated with the mechanical systems." [26] Architects often handle this problem by designing a passive system for half of the energy load and using mechanical systems to handle extreme conditions.

Robert Campbell maintains that lobbying by lighting engineers and manufacturers and others concerned with electricity has led to an increase in average lighting levels to what technicians call 200-foot candles, where only 40 is adequate. Today, lighting levels are receding, sometimes with the help of photovoltaic cells. Although extremely expensive, these cells allow lights to go on automatically when the light level drops below a certain point and off when natural light levels rise.[27]

Energy-efficient commercial structures already have been built in a number of cities. Shorter than skyscrapers, they have less exterior wall and roof surface exposed to the elements. Thus, less heat escapes in winter and penetrates in summer. For the same reason, windows generally are smaller and coated with sun-reflecting materials. One often-mentioned group of energy-efficient office buildings was commissioned for the state of California by Gov. Edmund G. Brown Jr. The group includes six office complexes in Sacramento and state buildings in Santa Rosa, San Jose, Van Nuys, Long Beach and Oakland. The first building, which won a citation in *Progressive Architecture's* 1979 awards program,[28] is located in Sacramento and goes by the name "Site 1-A." It incorporates a series of decks, which, combined with orange fabric shades and wood panels, give the building an air of informality. Sensing devices control the shades on the east and west, rolling them up to allow views or down to shut out sunlight throughout the day. Concrete trellis planks shade parts of the building's south side in summer. On the north there is no shading at all.

The 150-foot by 144-foot atrium is the building's most prominent feature. It contains tables and chairs that draw people at lunchtime as well as pedestrians from nearby buildings on their way to or from parking or bus stops. The atrium also redistrib-

---

[26] Flavin, *op cit.*, p. 34.

[27] Photovoltaic cells, also known as solar cells, have been used in America's space program for many years to provide energy in satellites. The cells consist mainly of two thin layers of material, one of them a semiconductor such as silicon and the other a metal such as aluminum or silver. A semiconductor can be treated so that when light strikes it electrons flow across the two layers — the so-called photovoltaic effect — and generate current. This current is drawn off in wires to operate electric motors, light bulbs or other devices.

[28] *Progressive Architecture* is published by Reinhold Publishing Co. in New York City. See Jim Murphy, "State Intentions," *Progressive Architecture*, August 1981, for a description of Site 1-A with photographs and illustrations.

utes heat and provides natural light, is a place for public performances and provides a large, serene space that adds some
elegance to the building. The atrium is topped by large angled
clerestories[29] punctuated by skylights facing north. South-facing vertical movable louvres (fin-like constructions) keep direct
sun out of the atrium in summer, while the skylights continue to
let in light. Winter sun is allowed to penetrate. Banner screens
are also lowered in winter to bounce sunlight into the atrium.
Large vertical canvas tubes equipped with fans recirculate
atrium air. "In the summer," Jim Murphy wrote in the August
1981 issue of *Progressive Architecture,* "the atrium is purged by
bringing cool night air down large air shafts and releasing heat
through skylight vents."

Ceilings in most of the office areas combine the building's
exposed concrete structure with suspended acoustical baffles.
The concrete absorbs heat from the lights, office machines and
people. During the night outside air is brought in to further
purge the interior of accumulated heat. Two rock-bed storage
chambers under the atrium each contain 660 tons of rocks that
store heat pumped in or out by reversible fans. Hot water is
heated by 2,000 square feet of solar collectors.

Adapting Old Buildings to Save Energy

Part of the push behind the preservation movement has been
the recognition that more energy can be saved by adapting old
buildings than by tearing them down and building new ones.
"Generally speaking, more energy is spent in building a building
than is spent in operating it for many years afterward," Robert
Campbell said in a recent interview. "So every existing building
is a kind of bank of energy that has already been expended." To
take advantage of this energy pool, homeowners and architects
are learning how to improve the energy efficiency of existing
structures. "Though it is a more difficult, costly, and institu-
tionally complex process than starting from scratch at the design stage, potential fuel savings from such a program in most
countries are greater than for the most ambitious new construction programs," Christopher Flavin wrote. "This is particularly
true in parts of Europe where very few new buildings will be
started over the next couple of decades." [30]

Conventional conservation measures in millions of homes in
North America and Europe have often reduced fuel bills by 10
percent or more, Flavin said. Researchers at the Princeton
(N.J.) Center for Energy and Environmental Studies found that
with an even more comprehensive program fuel bills could be

---

[29] A clerestory is an outside wall that rises above an adjoining roof and contains windows.
[30] Flavin, *op cit.,* p. 35.

reduced by two-thirds. In the late 1970s, the center experimented with 30 New Jersey townhouses; they added storm doors, developed new and more efficient storm windows and fitted some windows with insulated shutters to be closed at night. The Center's investigators also used a tracer test and infrared scan to locate remaining sources of air infiltration, which were then caulked and weatherstripped. The key to the success of the Princeton program was the thorough evaluation of each house's energy performance the researchers conducted beforehand. They found, for example, that leaks in many attics were causing warm air to bypass the insulation, one reason why attempts to add insulation to an existing building often do not result in much improvement. Flavin believes that effective retrofit programs require trained personnel to evaluate a building's performance and then specify a range of cost-effective solutions.

Some builders and homeowners have gone even further and converted conventional buildings into passive solar ones that use sunlight, shading and natural ventilation to provide most of the heating, cooling and lighting requirements. This is most feasible when buildings are properly positioned and landscaped. The most common kind of passive solar retrofit is a solar greenhouse that can be attached to a south side of a building without replacing any walls. Vents are often placed in the walls and fans added to circulate the captured heat. Solar greenhouses have become one of the most popular methods of home improvement in the United States; thousands were built during the late 1970s and now several firms market prefabricated greenhouses, making it possible to "solarize" a house for $2,000 to $3,000.

More complex retrofits have often proved successful for old commercial buildings, such as schools, factories and warehouses. Many of these in the Northeast have uninsulated south-facing brick walls, which are ideal for conversion to Trombe walls (created by adding glazing just outside the south-facing masonry wall).

Although the move to retrofit existing buildings has been widespread in recent years,[31] many architects believe that energy's major impact on architecture will be in the form of more regional, climate-sensitive design. Whatever the impact, the glass boxes of modern architecture are on their way out. While the alternatives do not please everyone, architects seem determined to break new ground by plundering the old.

---

[31] Almost 20 million homes — a quarter of the nation's housing stock — have been retrofitted with attic insulation since 1973, according to Christopher Flavin.

Selected Bibliography

Books

Blake, Peter, *Form Follows Fiasco: Why Modern Architecture Hasn't Worked*, Little, Brown, 1977.

Jencks, Charles A., *The Language of Post-Modern Architecture*, Academy Editions, 1977.

Goldberger, Paul, *The Skyscraper*, Knopf, 1981.

Stern, Robert A. M., *New Directions in American Architecture*, George Braziller, 1977.

Thorndike, Joseph J. Jr., ed., *Three Centuries of Notable American Architects*, American Heritage, Scribners, 1981.

Wolfe, Tom, *From Bauhaus to Our House*, Farrar Straus Giroux, 1981.

Articles

A.I.A. Journal (published by the American Institute of Architects), selected issues.

Architectural Record, selected issues.

Art in America, selected issues.

Goldberger, Paul, "The New American Skyscraper," *The New York Times Magazine*, Nov. 8, 1981.

Huxtable, Ada Louise, "Is Modern Architecture Dead?" *The New York Review of Books*, July 16, 1981.

"Restoration of Things Past," *Newsweek*, March 23, 1981.

Sporkin, Elizabeth, "Victoriana Is Back," *The Washingtonian*, December 1981.

"State Intentions," *Progressive Architecture*, August 1981.

Ward, Andrew, "The Trouble With Architects: The Bird's-eye Syndrome," *Atlantic*, May 1980.

Wiseman, Carter, "Room at the Tops," *New York*, Dec. 21, 1981.

Reports and Studies

Editorial Research Reports: "New Directions in Architecture," 1973 Vol. II, p. 903.

Flavin, Christopher, "Energy and Architecture: The Solar and Conservation Potential," Worldwatch Institute, 1980.

Cover illustration by Staff Artist
Robert Redding

Advances in Athletic Training

by

Marc Leepson

Jan. 27
1984

ADVANCES IN
ATHLETIC TRAINING

EVER SINCE Coroebus won the first Olympic foot race in 776 B.C., athletes have been searching for ways to improve their performance. Coroebus trained by running up and down hills. Milo of Croton, a 6th century B.C. Olympic wrestling champion, is said to have lifted a calf over his head daily until the animal was fully grown. Athletic training has come a long way since the days of the ancient Greeks. In the last 10 years alone, a combination of technological advances and burgeoning interest in physical fitness has revolutionized athletic training. Athletes from around the world will show off the benefits of these new training techniques when the XIV Olympic Winter Games begin Feb. 7 in Sarajevo, Yugoslavia.

"We're in an explosion of knowledge and there's an explosion of interest" in all aspects of sports training, said A. Garth Fisher, director of the Human Performance Research Center at Utah's Brigham Young University.[1] Coaches and athletes from professional to junior high school levels have at their disposal an extensive array of new training methods and athletic equipment to help athletes maximize their abilities and minimize injuries. These developments also have contributed to "an upward revision of the limits of performance," said sports analyst John Jerome, adding that they are "rising at a startling rate." [2]

Many of these training techniques are outgrowths of a relatively new medical discipline, sports medicine, which applies scientific knowledge to both the physical and mental aspects of athletic performance. "In most countries other than the United States when somebody talks about sports medicine they primarily are talking about sports orthopedics — orthopedic medicine dealing with sports injuries," said William Haskell, associate professor of medicine at the Stanford University School of Medicine and current president of the American College of Sports Medicine. But in the United States, Haskell said, "much more of the group is involved in the physiology and biochemistry, kineseology and biomechanics aspects of exercise and performance. People who consider themselves involved

---

[1] Fisher is co-author of *Scientific Basis of Athletic Conditioning* (1980). Remarks by Fisher and others quoted in this report, unless otherwise indicated, come from interviews with the author from Dec. 7-16.
[2] John Jerome, *The Sweet Spot in Time* (1980), pp. 28, 30.

with sports medicine generally are not the teachers out teaching physical education. They're more interested in the scientific basis or applications."

Sports Medicine's Latest Achievements

A list of some of sports medicine's accomplishments clearly illustrates the diversity of the discipline:

• Computerized scanners used by neurologists can evaluate head injuries rapidly and accurately.

• The widespread use of eye, mouth, head, face and ear protectors in sports such as hockey, racquetball, baseball, football, wrestling and skiing has prevented tens of thousands of injuries and millions of dollars of medical expenses annually.[3]

• Carbohydrate-loading, in which athletes who need to expend energy for long periods of time ingest large amounts of foods containing high energy-producing carbohydrates prior to competing, is "a milestone in sports nutrition and has significantly contributed to improved endurance performances," according to Haskell.[4]

• The widespread acceptance of the aerobic exercise concept, developed primarily by Dr. Kenneth H. Cooper, has helped athletes and non-athletes attain cardiovascular fitness.[5]

New tools for treating athletic injuries also have been developed. One of the most successful of these is the arthroscope, a fiber-optical device orthopedic surgeons use to diagnose and treat soft-tissue injuries, primarily torn knee cartilage or ligaments. Before the arthroscope, an injured knee often meant a premature end to an athlete's career. Even exploratory surgery was risky. But since the arthroscope came into widespread use in the late seventies, orthopedists have been able to examine injured knees without major surgery and to treat injuries much more effectively. The arthroscope is "one of the most significant developments for the care of athletes," said Dr. John Bergfeld, an orthopedic surgeon and president-elect of the American College of Sports Medicine. "It's something we can look inside a knee joint with and many times do surgery where we would have had to open up the knee before. But now we can remove the

---

[3] Hockey face protectors, for example, are now worn by more than 1.2 million players in the United States and Canada, according to ophthalmologist Paul F. Vigner, who chairs the eye safety committee of the American Society for Testing and Materials. Face protectors, Dr. Vigner said, prevent "70,000 eye and face injuries annually," resulting in "savings of $10 million in medical expenses." See "Sports Medicine: The Momentum Continues," *The Physician and Sportsmedicine*, June 1983, p. 156.

[4] Writing in *Runner's World*, December 1983, p. 34.

[5] Aerobic exercises — the slow, steady, non-stop regimens such as jogging or running, walking, swimming, cycling and dancing — help the entire cardiovascular system work more efficiently. After several months of steady aerobic training the heart muscles build up, allowing the heart to pump increased amounts of freshly oxygenated blood rapidly with each beat. See Kenneth H. Cooper, *Aerobics* (1968) and "Staying Healthy," *E.R.R.*, 1983 Vol. II, pp. 633-652.

torn portion of a cartilage or at least make a definitive diagnosis without having to make a big cut in the knee."

Lifting weights to build strength has been part of the training for some sports since the time of the ancient Greeks. But until the early seventies relatively few athletes worked with weights. "People felt that lifting made you 'muscle-bound,' that you got big, bulging muscles which a swimmer, say, certainly didn't want to have," said Bergfeld. Today, however, athletes from sports as diverse as swimming, track and field, baseball, golf, gymnastics and football use weight training. "When I first started pumping iron [six years ago] I was the only runner in the gym," said Laura DeWald, a 26-year-old long-distance runner who has qualified for the U.S. women's Olympic marathon trials. "It was really unusual to see runners in the weight room then. It was mostly football players. But a lot of runners have now realized that it is a necessary part of their training. Of the runners I know ... almost all of them lift weights." As Bergfeld put it: "Now almost every athlete, no matter what his or her discipline, lifts weights to gain muscle strength. . . ." Weight training is even popular among professional dancers, who had avoided lifting weights

Working out on a Nautilus machine

in the past. Bergfeld estimated that about half of all professional dancers work with weights.

Some athletes still work with conventional barbells and dumbbells ("free weights"), but many athletes, dancers and physical fitness devotees use recently developed weightlifting equipment, including sophisticated electromechanical devices such as the Orthrotron and the Cybex and weight machines such as the Nautilus and Universal Gym. These devices allow athletes to concentrate on building strength in specific muscles in a manner that approximates the movements of their particular sports. Athletes in general do not work with heavy weights. "The heavily muscled bodybuilder usually lifts large amounts of weights through few repetitions, say four to five," said Dr. Bergfeld, who is team physician for the Cleveland Browns of the National Football League. "Whereas for the lean, elongated muscles in the dancer or the swimmer, they lift lighter weights, say 20 repetitions. And they don't do as much. A bodybuilder will spend his whole workout lifting weights. But it's only one part of [training for] a runner or a football or baseball player."

Controversy Over Anabolic Steroid Use

There is another, more controversial side to today's science-based athletic training revolution. Many athletes, including football players, weight lifters and track and field athletes, take anabolic steroids (the various synthetic derivatives of the male hormone testosterone) to try to build strength and improve their performance. Athletes discovered using steroids — as well as other drugs that affect athletic performance such as amphetamines and some narcotics — are ineligible to compete in events sanctioned by the U.S. Olympic Committee (USOC), the International Olympic Committee (IOC) and virtually every other amateur and professional sports governing authority.

Steroids not only provide an artificial boost to athletic performance, but they also can cause severe health problems. "Unfortunately, the healthy athlete who takes these drugs may not recognize the adverse reaction, or allows irreversible damage to take place," wrote sports medicine specialists Max Novich and Buddy Taylor.[6] Researchers have linked heavy steroid use to enlarged prostate glands, testicular atrophy, sterilization and liver damage. No one knows, moreover, what the long-term effects of heavy steroid use might be.

Despite the potential sanctions and health risks, athletes continue to abuse steroids. A scandal that broke at last summer's Pan American Games in Caracas, Venezuela, brought worldwide attention to the problem. Twelve athletes from eight countries — 11 weight lifters including gold-medal winner Jeff Michels of the United States and one cyclist — were disqualified from the games after tests found they had taken anabolic steroids or testosterone. Twelve U.S. track and field athletes left the games rather than submit to the tests. The incident illustrated the widespread use of steroids. "I've watched what was at first a 'secret' drug known only to a handful of elite weight lifters become a phenomenon so widespread that a majority of recent Olympic athletes, male and female, in track and field and the strength sports are believed to have used some form of steroid," wrote former weight lifter Terry Todd. "[It is] a phenomenon so widespread that pro football players have told me that as many as 50 percent of the active NFL linemen and linebackers have used steroids with the intent of improving their performance; a phenomenon so widespread that reports surface from

---

[6] Max M. Novich and Buddy Taylor, *Training and Conditioning of Athletes* (1970), p. 130.

Sports Medicine Glossary

Arthroscopy — Surgical examination of the interior of a joint with an arthroscope, a small instrument using fiber-optic technology. The procedure is performed most commonly on the knee.

Biomechanics — The study of human movement, primarily using high-speed cameras, computers and special analytical systems. The idea is to help athletes understand the mechanics of the body and how they relate to sports performance.

Exercise Physiology — The study of anatomical and physiological factors that affect performance. Sports physiologists measure athletes' heart and lung endurance and capacity, muscular strength, joint flexibility and percentage of body fat. This can help determine an athlete's strengths and weaknesses and identify what training programs will enhance his performance.

Kinesiology — The study of the principles of mechanics and anatomy in relation to human movement.

Sports Psychology — Training involving any of the myriad mental aspects of sports.

---

time to time of teen-agers being advised by their high school, or even junior high school coaches to take steroids." [7]

Taking drugs to try to improve performance is nothing new for athletes. In the early days of professional boxing, for example, fighters took substances such as strychnine tablets, spirits of ammonia, brandy and even champagne before and during fights. Some boxers had a cocaine-enriched ointment massaged into their skin and face before a bout so they would be anesthetized against pain. Long-distance cyclists in the first decades of the century ingested coffee, tea, caffeine tablets and narcotics such as cocaine and heroin to give them a boost during races. They also drank excessive amounts of alcohol during rest periods. [8]

Although there are sporadic reports of athletes using stimulants such as amphetamines and some narcotic pain killers, steroids are causing the biggest problems in sports today. [9] Anabolic steroids were developed to help heal muscular problems; the steroids induce a building up (anabolic) process within the

---

[7] Writing in *Sports Illustrated*, Aug. 1, 1983, p. 64.

[8] For background see Novich and Taylor, *op. cit.*, pp. 120-124.

[9] Sports medicine practitioners are beginning to voice concerns about a recently developed and potentially harmful "performance enhancing" substance known as synthetic human growth hormone used to treat dwarfism. Some parents reportedly have administered the growth hormone to their normal-sized children in the belief the substance will make them "bigger or more competitive," said Melvin M. Grumback, chairman of the pediatrics department at the University of California at San Francisco. "I'm concerned about a lot of unknown effects" of the hormone on normal children, Dr. Grumback told *The Chronicle of Higher Education* recently. He said that excessive amounts of the growth hormone may cause a mild diabetic condition, impaired nerve function and abnormal enlargement of the nose, jaw or fingers.

body, promoting tissue repair and muscle growth. The first anabolic steroid produced was Dianabol, manufactured by Ciba Pharmaceutical Co. in the late 1950s.

Athletes, mostly weight lifters, soon began taking steroids in the belief that they helped build muscles and increase strength. But scientific research has not yet determined how steroids affect athletic performance. Researchers now believe their effect may be only indirect, causing physiological and psychological changes that induce users to work harder to increase strength. "When all the objective evidence is considered ... it would appear that steroids administered for 3 to 6 weeks often contribute to extra gains in strength, body weight, and lean body mass, if the recipients participate simultaneously in a program of intensive strength training," the authors of one athletic training textbook wrote.[10]

The International Amateur Athletic Federation now requires athletes who break world records to submit to tests for steroids and other drugs; it recently suspended seven athletes for life after they failed the tests. The USOC has been criticized for laxity in dealing with the steroid problem. But in the wake of the Pan American Games crackdown, the USOC instituted its own testing program using the sophisticated detection devices employed for the first time in Caracas. The mandatory tests already have been given on a random basis to U.S. athletes at competitions around the country. In the last three months of 1983, for example, tests were conducted on athletes at the U.S. Amateur Boxing Championships in Colorado Springs, Colo., and among weight lifters and ice hockey players. The USOC has announced it will test every American athlete at each Olympic trial competition for 100 substances, including steroids, banned by the International Olympic Committee.

Olympic Training Role

THE AMATEUR Athletic Act of 1978, which was based on the recommendations of a presidential commission on amateur sports set up by President Ford in 1975, considerably broadened the power of the U.S. Olympic Committee. In addition to its existing responsibility for sending teams to the quadrennial Olympic games, the USOC was also "set up as the

---

[10] Clayne R. Jensen and A. Garth Fisher, *Scientific Basis of Athletic Conditioning* (1979), p. 256.

Olympic Training Center in Colorado Springs

central coordinating body for amateur sports in the United States," said Mike Moran, the committee's director of communications. "The old theory used to be that once every four years we picked an Olympic team and sent it off to the games. But in between there was nothing going on. . . . We are now an organization of opportunity rather than a travel agency." [11]

As part of its new responsibilities, the USOC has undertaken several programs that have direct impact on sports training. For one thing, the committee works very closely with the 28 amateur sports federations, known as national governing bodies (NGBs). Under the 1978 law, the NGBs were assigned day-to-day management and development of their sports nationwide. The USOC provides direct grants to the NGBs and encourages them to use the facilities at the Olympic Training Center in Colorado Springs, Colo. Seventeen NGBs have moved their national headquarters to the training center site. "We give them free space, services, computer time and all the things necessary for their functioning," Moran said. "The idea is to make this the amateur sports capital of the United States. . . . We've [also] offered them all the services and room and board for their athletes if they want to come here. . . . It's centralizing the amateur sports family."

The 34-acre, 20-building site at the foot of Pike's Peak that Colorado Springs donated to the USOC in 1976 was once headquarters for the North American Air Defense Command. A second training center, at Lake Placid, N.Y., opened in November 1982 to work with athletes in sports contested in the winter Olympics. Some 20,000 athletes from 30 sports trained at the

[11] The act also settled a long-running feud between the Amateur Athletic Union and the National Collegiate Athletic Association over control of amateur athletics in the United States. The dispute at times had prevented the best American athletes from participating in international competitions, including the Olympics. The 1978 law essentially stripped these bodies of their power to oversee amateur sports (except at the intercollegiate level) and gave most of that authority to the USOC and the individual sports' national governing bodies. See 1978 *CQ Almanac*, pp. 795-796 and section on U.S. amateur athletic problems in "Olympics 1976," *E.R.R.*, 1976 Vol. II, pp. 509-514.

two centers in 1983; about 100 weight lifters, cyclists, race walkers, judo athletes and boxers live at Colorado Springs on a permanent basis. They receive free room and board and work with their coaches and trainers at the center's facilities. The Colorado Springs training center's newest facility is a $4 million sports center that opened in July 1982. The facility contains six gymnasiums and has training facilities for archery, basketball, boxing, fencing, gymnastics, judo, table tennis, team handball, volleyball, weightlifting and wrestling.

Among the USOC's training programs is a special $2 million program called Operation Gold. About 400 athletes, including 30-35 members of the boxing team, are taking part in the program, which began in 1981. The boxers live and train with their coaching staff at the Colorado Springs training facility; the younger members of the team attend high school in the city. Others in the program who prefer to do most or all of their training at home, such as world champion runner Mary Decker, receive more than $5,000 a year to help offset training costs.

The USOC, whose current four-year budget is $80.5 million, receives no funding from the federal government. About 40 percent of its budget comes from donations from American corporations; the balance is made up of public contributions and proceeds from benefit concerts, fund-raising dinners and other special programs. More than 30 large corporate donors have become official USOC sponsors. Miller Brewing Co., for example, is the Colorado Springs center's primary benefactor. The company's $3 million donation accounts for about two-thirds of the training center's budget.

Evolution of Sports Medicine Program

The 1978 Amateur Sports Act also mandated that the USOC become involved in sports medicine. "With the Amateur Sports Act, sports medicine science became one of the focal points of how to improve our athletes' performance," said Dr. Irving Dardik of the USOC Sports Medicine Council. "So the USOC as a governing body then took it upon itself to develop this whole program." Dardik, a vascular surgeon, was chosen to design the USOC's sports medicine program, which is administered by Kenneth Clarke, a former college dean who became director of the USOC's sports medicine division in Colorado Springs in

July 1981. The USOC program "combines the traditional clinical concerns of sports medicine — both prevention and treatment of athletic injuries and illnesses — with the sports sciences in helping guide the athletes' goal to enhance performance through legitimate training techniques," Clarke said. "That includes physiology, biomechanics, psychology, nutrition, vision, dental concerns and so on."

The Colorado Springs program has four basic components: a medical clinic, a biomechanics laboratory, a sports physiology facility and an educational program. The clinic's physician and three athletic trainers provide a wide range of medical assistance, including in-depth physical examinations and dental care, to the athletes who train at the center. The clinic also is charged with overseeing the USOC's drug control program.

The biomechanics and sports physiology departments *(see glossary, p. 167)* are involved primarily in research, evaluating athletes and athletic preformance. Among the sophisticated comupters and photographic equipment in use in the biomechanics laboratory is a "force platform," that uses computer-analyzed videotape to show lifters exactly how their weight is distributed during a lift. "When he lifts a weight, within 15 seconds he has a full picture [of computerized 'stick figures'] of how he did it, said Clarke.[12]

The USOC's sports medicine education services include a variety of programs for physicians, coaches and athletes. Seminars, workshops and conferences are conducted throughout the country. "The sports medicine program is not just Colorado Springs," Clarke said. "The rest is linking with sports medicine people and laboratories around the country where the athletes are so they don't have to come here. We are trying to find ways of extending our services as efficiently as possible to where the clusters of athletes in given sports may be. We're also encouraging and helping the national governing bodies to develop sports medicine committees of their own. . . ."

Elite Athlete and Youth Talent Projects

Sports medicine at the USOC also includes several programs under the heading of "special projects," such as weight training,

---

[12] Quoted in *The Wall Street Journal*, Sept. 9, 1983.

sports psychology, nutrition counseling and vision evaluation. In addition, eight national governing bodies are working with the USOC in a special Elite Athlete project to help NGBs identify and develop athletes of world-class caliber. The eight federations are working on individual programs, and the USOC Sports Medicine Council has a team of sports medicine specialists designing a program that all 28 Olympic NGBs could use in a united effort to find and train elite athletes. "We already know what aspects of sports medicine we're going to concentrate on and what technologies we're going to use" in this program, Dr. Dardik said. "They're highly advanced technologies that are not currently being applied."

Among the new training technologies are a computerized electrical muscle stimulation system and an advanced type of biofeedback system based on cardiac rhythms and pulse monitoring. The latter device will allow an athlete to monitor his or her pulse during exercise. "Without any wires you can see your pulse during a very heavy workout on your wrist with accuracy," said Dr. Dardik. "You have your pulse fed back to you on an average of every 30 seconds for over an hour. We can correlate that with [other] measurements and the athlete can then train and know when he . . . should be stopping. We're going to be implementing that particularly with endurance types of events, cycling and so forth."

Another special project set to debut soon is the USOC's Youth Talent Search. The idea is eventually to set up a nationwide educational, testing and monitoring system — using new sports medicine techniques — to steer children between the ages of 11 and 16 into Olympic sports to which they are physiologically and psychologically suited. No such system exists today, even though most sports medicine analysts see a need for one. "We don't look at kids and put them into activities," said Fisher of Brigham Young University's Human Performance Research Center. "For instance, some kid weighs 110 pounds and he wants to go out for football. They give him some pads, and he gets beat up. I think our coaches ought to be more aware of which kids fit where. . . . You can run them down a track and if they have natural speed, then you can start encouraging them in some speed events, and so forth."

The USOC's Youth Talent Search is scheduled to begin pilot programs in several cities this spring. Talent search teams, consisting of coaches, trainers and athletes of selected Olympic sports, will hold three-day programs focusing on several sports. "We will show youngsters what the sports are all about and do some simple testing on them — anything from reaction time to concentration time to measurements of a few different param-

The Body Clock, Time and Performance

There is a growing awareness in the sports community that scientific research has something practical to offer athletes. The U.S. Olympic Committee (USOC), for example, is underwriting a medical research project at Brigham and Women's Hospital of the Harvard Medical School on how the body's circadian rhythms (the "biological clock") affect athletic performance. "The study will assess the impact of circadian variations on athletic performance," said Dr. Charles Czeisler, the project's director, who heads the hospital's neuroendocrinology laboratory. "We want to see the relationship of those variations to ... the timing of other performance cycles and a variety of other different physiologic functions that vary with the day and the night."

The project will use a computerized exercise machine to monitor and compare athletic performance over long periods of time. "This relates to issues such as the adaptation of athletes following the transition across time zones," Czeisler said. "For example, when they have to go to Sarajevo to compete in the Winter Olympic Games they have to adjust to a five or six or seven hour difference depending on where they're coming from.... We're trying to understand first of all if it matters to athletic performance and if so what strategies might be developed to facilitate an adaptation like that." The project, which began in November 1983, is not expected to be completed until late 1984.

eters of physiology," said Dr. Dardik. "The kids would have the opportunity to see what the sports are about, to see if they might be pretty good at this one or that one. It's different than picking a four-foot-tall kid and putting him in a basketball program. Maybe he'd be better off in gymnastics." Eventually, the USOC hopes to use computers to link children interested in Olympic sports with nearby training facilities and coaches.

Challenge from Communist Countries

It is no secret that the U.S. Olympic Committee's recent push to develop innovative sports medicine programs has been influenced by the recent successes of Eastern bloc countries — primarily the Soviet Union and German Democratic Republic (East Germany) — in international competition. Since 1952, when the Soviet Union first entered the Olympic Games, the Russians have won more medals than any other nation. In the 1976 summer games, East Germany won 40 gold medals; six more than the United States. In the 1980 games, which the United States boycotted because of the Soviet invasion of Afghanistan, the Soviet Union won an unprecedented 197 medals, including 80 golds. Most observers agree that American sports medicine is on a par with sports medicine in the Soviet

Union and in East Germany. But the communist countries have evolved highly efficient centralized national programs to groom athletes for international competition. "Scientists who have traveled widely among Eastern European countries say there is not so much an athletic gap as there is an application gap," said sports analyst Jerome. "We know what they know, we're just not using it yet."[13] It was East Germany's success in 1976, in fact, that convinced the USOC to get involved in sports medicine. "I'd say that a turning point was 1976 when the East Germans [bested the United States in gold medals] at the Montreal Olympics," Dr. Dardik said. "The interest in sports medicine science has really taken hold since then."

The Soviet Union's push for the competitive edge began shortly after World War II when the country instituted a program to catch up with and overtake the western industrialized nations in international sports competitions. "As in other spheres, the incentive to produce top results was ... the awarding of cash prizes and priorities in the allocation of flats and scarce commodities for setting records and winning championships," wrote James Riordan, an expert on Soviet sports. "All athletes ... received salaries and bonuses according to their sports ranking, thus further encouraging the formation of an elite of sport stars."[14] It has been well documented that one of the communist countries' primary advantages in international amateur competition is the fact that they do not have any "professional" athletes. Nearly all of the Soviet Union's world-class athletes are described as students, members of the armed forces or physical education instructors. Most work for the state; training is their full-time job.

The Soviet equivalent of the USOC is the Physical Culture and Sport Committee of the Council of Ministers of the U.S.S.R., known as the Sports Committee. This state-financed body employs coaches and their staffs and is responsible for locating promising Olympians and steering them into one of the nation's elite athletic training institutions. Among the committee's programs is the genetic testing of infants to try to identify potential world-class athletes. Moscow's State Physical Culture Institute has been involved with this testing program for more than a decade. "We are working out a method for very early forecasting of athletic ability, even in the first year of life on the basic of genetic markers," said Prof. Boris Nikityuk. "Our objective is to direct kids into sports they are physically best suited for and avoid sports that would not be good for them."[15]

[13] Jerome, *op. cit.*, p. 239.
[14] James Riordan, *Sports in Soviet Society* (1978), p. 162.
[15] Quoted in *USA Today*, Feb. 17, 1983.

USOC officials say that their goals extend beyond helping U.S. athletes win Olympic medals. "The main goal of the organization as a whole is to provide more opportunities and funding for athletes from the grass-roots level to handicapped to seniors ... and to promote amateur sports in the United States, as well as produce Olympic teams," said Mike Moran. Nevertheless, it appears as if the USOC's beefed-up sports medicine and training programs are at least partially responsible for recent improvements by American athletes in international competition. American athletes fared especially well at the 1983 Pan American Games and at the August 1983 World Track and Field Championships in Helsinki, Finland.[16] The United States now has the strongest amateur women's basketball, women's volleyball and women's field hockey teams that it has ever put together, and other teams and individuals are favored to win gold medals in both this year's winter and summer Olympics. F. Don Miller, the USOC's executive director, predicts that the U.S. Olympic team and individual performances at this summer's games, which begin July 28 in Los Angeles, "will be the best in the history of the country." [17]

New Applications Used

THE FIELD of sports psychology is growing rapidly, and all indications are that this discipline will be an increasingly important branch of sports medicine. "I believe that the records that will be broken in the future will not be broken by better training or more training," said Rainer Martens, sports psychologist for the U.S. Olympic Nordic ski team. "I think they'll be broken by better psychological preparation." Haskell of the American College of Sports Medicine recently predicted "major growth in the area of sports psychology." The field, Haskell said, "is still in its infancy. I expect that within the next 10 years we'll see more accurate methods developed for measuring the impact of exercise on our minds. It will also be interesting to see how the psychiatric community deals with the opposite question: how our mental status influences our exercise

[16] U.S. athletes won 24 medals in Helsinki, one more than the Soviet Union and two more than East Germany.

[17] Quoted in *The Wall Street Journal*, Sept. 9, 1983. Possible gold medal winners at the winter games include skier Phil Mahre and skaters Rosalynn Sumners and Scott Hamilton. Americans considered possible gold medal winners at the Los Angeles Olympics this summer include sprinter and long jumper Carl Lewis, hurdler Edwin Moses, pole vaulter Billy Olson, discus thrower Ben Plucknett, diver Greg Luganis, marathon runner Alberto Salazar, middle-distance runner Mary Decker, sprinter Evelyn Ashford, heptathlete Jane Frederick, swimmers Tracy Caulkins, Mary T. Meagher and Tiffany Cohen and gymnasts Bart Conner, Peter Vidmar, Mary Lou Retton and Julianne McNamara.

performance.... The concept of concentration is going to be extremely important to athletes over the next decade." [18]

Sports psychology is not certified as a discipline by the American Psychological Association. One reason is that sports psychology is primarily involved with teaching athletes how best to use their mental abilities rather than with helping emotionally disturbed athletes. "Sports psychology deals with the mental aspects of sports," said Craig Wrisberg, a physical education professor at the University of Tennessee and treasurer of the North American Society for the Psychology of Sport and Physical Activity.[19] "It deals with anything from a strategy I might use to run a race ... to what I'm thinking about when I'm trying to high jump ... to coping with anxiety, the fear of failure that affects athletes' concentration."

Many practicing sports psychologists, Wrisberg said, are not licensed psychologists. "They are people out of a physical education background who have some type of doctoral degree in physical education. They understand sport. They've taken course work in counseling methods and usually in cognitive areas of psychology." Rainer Martens, for example, is a physical education professor at the University of Illinois. "I'm not a clinical psychologist," Martens said. "I feel that what I do is work as an educational sports psychologist. I'm a teacher. Perhaps even more simply put, I'm a coach with the teams that I work with. I'm coaching. I'm teaching them psychological skills; whereas the other coaches are teaching them physical and training skills."

Martens has devised what he calls a psychological skills program. Starting with a five-day session during the off-season, he and his associates lead group discussions on the psychological aspects of sports performance and then meet individually with the athletes and coaches. The group discussions are necessary, Martens said, "because athletes are amazingly naive about those psychological factors operating in sports. The other [reason] is because this is an area that they feel uncomfortable in talking about with other athletes — or the coach. They just never discuss it." In the individual sessions Martens teaches imaging, a concentration and relaxation method. In imaging, "athletes who need to psych themselves up visualize themselves in and rehearse the competitive situation, while those who need to relax imagine some peaceful, calming scene," wrote Robert M. Nideffer, a professor at the California School of Professional Psychology in San Diego.[20]

---

[18] Writing in *Runner's World*, December 1983, p. 44.

[19] When the society was founded in 1966 it had 15 members. Membership today is more than 450.

[20] Robert M. Nideffer, *The Inner Athlete: Mind Plus Muscle for Winning* (1976), p. 188.

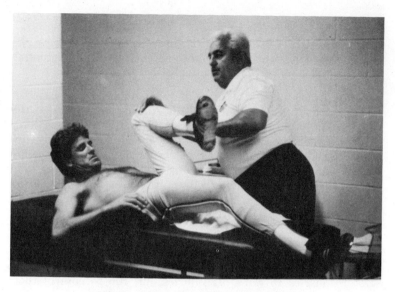

Baltimore Orioles trainer Ralph Salvon helps
pitcher Jim Palmer with leg stretching exercises.

Sports psychologists also use a variety of stress management techniques to help athletes. These include progressive relaxation exercises (*see below*), deep breathing, biofeedback, meditation, yoga and other types of stretching routines. "What we try to do is present the notion that there is an inverted 'U' curve relationship between performance and arousal or motivation," Martens said. "If you are not aroused enough, your performance won't be very good. But when you become too aroused, then you become stressed and your performance begins to decline. Athletes need to find that optimal arousal level for themselves.... We try to teach them how to become sensitive to these emotional experiences they're having in sport and to begin to discover that optimal level and teach them strategies for moving their arousal level up or down on that continuum."

Techniques Used in Professional Sports

Professional basketball, baseball, football and hockey teams are at the forefront in applying sports medicine techniques, including sports psychology. The Philadelphia Flyers of the National Hockey League, for example, employed Julie K. Anthony, a clinical psychologist and former world-class tennis player, in 1981-82. Among other things, Anthony taught the players progressive relaxation, a technique involving regular relaxation of the body's major muscles. "Practicing twice a day for 15 minutes, [a hockey player] eventually can take a few deep breaths, tense and relax a few muscles and feel his entire body relax," Anthony said. "In the game, if the score is close and he is waiting to go in, he can use this technique to keep himself from getting too tight. Or if he has just been involved in a brawl, he can skate around for a few seconds, use the relaxation technique and then be able to play effectively."

Some professional athletes, including major-league baseball players Rod Carew of the California Angels, Ron Kittle of the Chicago White Sox and Bill Buckner of the Chicago Cubs, have had success on the field after working with professional hypnotists. "Under hypnosis I was better able to talk about my batting motion and what I was doing wrong," said Buckner, who has worked with St. Paul, Minn., hypnotist Harvey Misel. "Then, when I was still hypnotized, Dr. Misel reminded me of things I should be working on." [21]

Other advances in sports medicine have caused significant changes in the way professional athletes train. More players than ever before work with weights to increase their strength, stretch muscles to ward off injuries and run to control their weight and build endurance. Teams employ strength or conditioning coaches, such as the Philadelphia Phillies' Gus Hoefling who specializes in calisthenics and relaxation exercises based on the Chinese martial art of kung fu. "Hoefling's gotten some of our players through some very bad times," said former Phillies owner Ruly Carpenter. "[Pitcher John] Denny's had one of his best seasons ever [in 1983]; he gives credit to Gus." [22]

Most of the NFL teams run comprehensive year-round training and medical programs starting with a thorough physical examination. "It used to be that the old physical exam was, 'Can you hear thunder and see lightning?'" said Dr. Bergfeld, the Browns' team physician. "Now they're pretty extensive. Most teams will do all sorts of sophisticated tests to find out what [the player's] real endurance is and strength and put athletes on specific programs where they find some weaknesses." The Browns' physical exam, Bergfeld said, also measures the players' percentage of body fat. "That way we know how much of their body is muscle, how much is fat. And we try to get them to an ideal body fat. It's different for different positions. So we counsel them on nutrition. We want to get them to a certain body weight based on physiologic formulas."

The Browns are expected to work out 12 months a year. Each player has a team-prescribed training program for the off-season, including running, weightlifting and agility exercises. "It's worked out scientifically," Bergfeld said. "We have a physiologist who sits down and works it out so ideally we know we're stressing the muscles the way we want to stress them for foot-

---

[21] Anthony and Buckner were quoted by Emily Greenspan in "Conditioning Athletes' Minds," *The New York Times Magazine*, Aug. 28, 1983, p. 34.
[22] Quoted in *Esquire*, January 1984, pp. 116-117.

ball performance.... We even lift weights during the season. We cut down on the amount, but we do it once a week to maintain their strength.... The well-conditioned athlete has less of a chance of injury than the poorer conditioned one."

Reaching Athletic Performance Limits

One of the unanswered questions about sports medicine is the extent of its influence on athletic performance. Is the breaking of a world record, for example, attributable to sports medicine, to the innate ability of the individual athlete, or to some combination of the two? The USOC's Dardik downplayed the importance of sports medicine. "You can't measure the success of sports medicine," he said. "I never want to see an athlete say, 'It was sports medicine that did it for me.' There's no such animal. The athlete did it. Sports medicine science is just [one of the] tools on the way." Sports analyst Jerome agreed. "In exercise physiology some very basic questions about training phenomena, about the production of energy and other aspects of the biochemistry of exercise are now becoming clearer," he wrote, "but none is going to make us start producing 3:40 milers, sub-two-hour marathoners, or nine-flat sprinters.... Most world records are broken by the smallest of measurable increments." [23]

William Haskell said that advances in training techniques have been responsible for some increases in athletic performances, but only in certain sports. In the strength and power events such as weightlifting and shotput throwing, Haskell said, new training methods have contributed directly to world-record performances. In other sports, he said, improvements in performance are due to advances in equipment design, including athletic shoes and track surfaces, and because there are more athletes than ever before. "If you have a broader base and you recruit more people, you're going to get better performances," Haskell said.

Sports psychologist Wrisberg stressed the importance of innate ability. "You can whip a mule all day and it's not going to win the Kentucky Derby," he said. Athletes who break world records, Wrisberg said, "have the propensity physiologically — maybe the right ratio of white to red muscle fibers for a sprinter, say — and they also have it psychologically.... If there is any learning or adaptation, I would suspect it is not all that great [and] in my opinion it's probably in the psychological realm." Whatever the reasons, few doubt that athletes today are

---

[23] Jerome, *op. cit.*, pp. 318-319. The world record for the mile, 3:47.33, was set by Sebastian Coe of Great Britain Aug. 28, 1981; for the marathon the record is 2:08.13, set by Alberto Salazar of the United States on Oct. 25, 1981; the record for the 100-meter dash is 9.93, set by American Calvin Smith on July 3, 1983.

generally in better shape than ever before and that athletic performances will continue to improve in the future. And there is little doubt that today's advanced training methods are at least partially responsible for the rise in the limits of human performance.

Selected Bibliography

Books

Anderson, Bob, *Stretching*, Shelter Publications, 1980.
Gallwey, Timothy, *The Inner Game of Tennis*, Random House, 1974.
Jensen, Clayne R. and A. Garth Fisher, *Scientific Basis of Athletic Conditioning*, Lea & Febiger, 1979.
Jerome, John, *The Sweet Spot in Time*, Summit Books, 1980.
Leepson, Marc, *Executive Fitness*, McGraw-Hill, 1983.
Leonard, George, *The Ultimate Athlete*, Viking, 1974.
Matveyev, L., *Fundamentals of Sports Training*, Progress Publishers, 1981.
McMaster, James H., *The ABCs of Sports Medicine*, Krieger Publishing, 1982.
Nideffer, Robert M., *The Inner Athlete: Mind Plus Muscle for Winning*, Crowell, 1976.
Novich, Max M. and Buddy Taylor, *Training and Conditioning of Athletes*, Lea & Febiger, 1970.
Riordan, James, *Sport in Soviet Society*, Cambridge University Press, 1978.
Ryan, Frank, *Sports and Psychology*, Prentice-Hall, 1981.

Articles

Greenspan, Emily, "Conditioning Athletes' Minds," *The New York Times Magazine*, Aug. 28, 1983.
Haskell, William, "Ten Years of Sportsmedicine," *Runner's World*, December 1983.
"Sports Medicine: The Momentum Continues," *The Physician and Sportsmedicine*, June 1983.
Seixas, Suzanne, "Going for the Gold," *Money*, December 1983.
Todd, Terry, "The Steroid Predicament," *Sports Illustrated*, Aug. 1, 1983.

Reports and Studies

Editorial Research Reports, "Staying Healthy," 1983 Vol. II, p. 633; "Physical Fitness Boom," 1978 Vol. I, p. 261; "Olympics 1976," 1976 Vol. II, p. 501.
United States Olympic Committee, "Doping Control: Questions and Answers," 1983.

Graphics: Cover illustration by Assistant Art Director Robert Redding; p. 165 photo courtesy Nautilus Virginia; p. 169 photo courtesy United States Olympic Committee; p. 177 photo courtesy Baltimore Orioles.

INDEX